Island Man
NAIVE BEGINNINGS
Andy Strangeway

Published in the United Kingdom in 2007 by
Andy Strangeway
1A Holly Close
Full Sutton
York
YO41 1LY

Printed and bound in the United Kingdom by
Publicity Print Marketing Ltd
Warrington WA3 5SW

FOR RUTH

Acknowledgements

I have been grateful for the help that the boatmen of these islands have given me. I would like to thank Jock, Kenny and especially Hamish for their assistance.

I would also like to say thank you to Grahame and Joy.

Where would I have been without the love and support of my wife Ruth?

Beyond those in the foreground, there are countless people who have helped me with a phone call, a contact or who have been there just for a yarn.

I am indebted to you all.

Contents

Appendix 1 – Map of Scotland

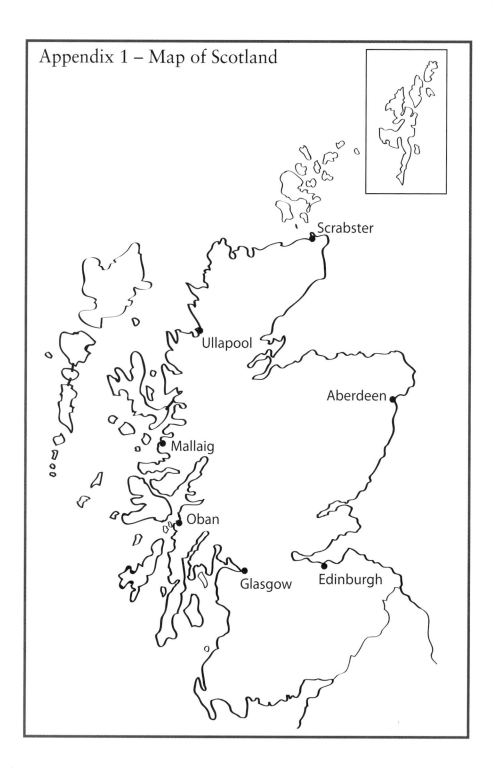

PREFACE

I was born in 1965 in Londesborough, a small village on the Yorkshire Wolds; moving from there at the age of three to Nunburnholme, a similar village, which is only three miles away. Here I was to live for the next 29 years.

My school days were definitely not the easiest. I wasn't thick and I wasn't clever and so, falling between the "thickies" and the "brain boxes," I seemed to spend most of my time alone. But the one thing I was good at was Chess. Being blessed with a brain that could feed things through quickly, meant that as a result, I was picked to play for the school chess team by the time I was 12.

Leaving school at 16, I started my working life amongst a team of estate workers who maintained the local village estate. Three years later, I handed in my notice and became a self-employed decorator, which I continue to this very day.

But, by the time I was 23, my feet were well and truly starting to itch and so, for the next nine years I never saw a winter on the Wolds; instead choosing to enjoy wild parties, beautiful girls and experience a new sense of adventure. India was to become a major part of my life and during my first trip there I became a vegetarian, packed in my 40 to 60 a day habit and learnt about Gandhi!

Aged 32, I decided to buy a small flat in the local town, knowing that I was just too young to move into an old folk's home with my parents; and it was at the same time that I met Ruth. The wanderlust remained with me however and over the next few years I continued to travel up to three months a year, with and without Ruth.

Then, having just returned from a trip to India, whilst Ruth and I were enjoying a few days in Dunoon with her wheelchair bound Aunt, I came across a book, which told of the 162 islands of Scotland, 40 hectares and above. It was at that moment my life changed forever. For me it was a major decision to buy the book; business was quiet and the book cost £25. But I removed my Yorkshireman's hat and bought it.

The adventure had begun. At that moment I really had no idea how it would unfold.
I ask you as the reader to understand that I have tried to capture my opinions and thoughts as they were at each stage of my journey. These may be about the

islands, people I have met, spiritual belief and life in general. Some or all of these opinions and thoughts may have changed, for like all human beings my mind is forever changing.

So come and join me on my journey to the islands of Scotland and of the opening of my soul.

"(Yorkshiremen are) richly endowed with that gritty determination, the wilful refusal to give up and the sheer bloody – mindedness that eventually prevails."

Bernard Ingham

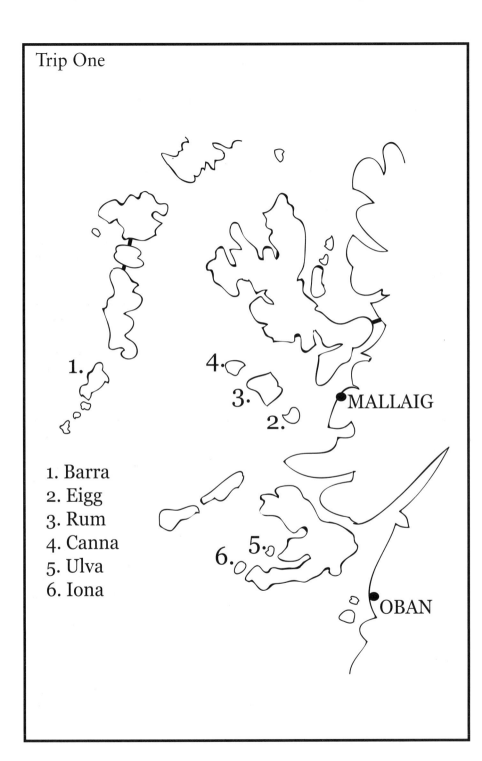

Trip One

1. Barra
2. Eigg
3. Rum
4. Canna
5. Ulva
6. Iona

MALLAIG

OBAN

I
NAIVE BEGINNINGS

FRIDAY 5TH SEPTEMBER 2003
TO TUESDAY 9TH SEPTEMBER 2003

My first trip starts early - 3.45am to be exact! This is because the taxi driver to York Station, my partner Ruth, has to be in Leeds by 7.00am. It's an emotional farewell, neither of us really knowing what lies ahead; yet it's just perfect and we part with a deep feeling of love.

Before we finally say goodbye Ruth takes the official "start of journey" photo. As usual I am breathing in! I am now weighing 77 kgs., 3 - 4kgs. heavier than I should be.
York Station seems very cold. I hope that the Outer Hebrides are not much colder. I have tried to keep my 38kgs. kit as small as possible, just one more layer, gloves and woolly hat, then I will freeze.

I really feel that I am going to do this! Watching the business travellers getting on and off trains, I realise just how free I am, I feel so elated! All my skills, all my experiences are now joining force, bringing me to what I feel will be the highlight and purpose of my life, so far. My journey to the islands, as well as being a physical journey, will be a journey of my mind, body and soul. If I manage to achieve peace in my mind then my body will be in harmony.

Travelling north to Glasgow via Edinburgh is a typical GNER / Scot Rail journey. It is only enlivened by a quick beer in Glasgow before I set off once more, this time for Oban. From here the scenery gets better and better. Unfortunately I don't see too much of it, the beer and the early morning start taking its toll, and the next thing I know I am waking up in Oban being greeted by the sight of the pier and a "Cal Mac" ferry! Oban is the most perfect of towns with 9,000 inhabitants. It can grow to 40,000 with the tourist influx. There is a lovely selection of tourists here, opening doors, polite and smiling. It is good to have arrived.

On account of my heavy load, I opt for the easy route to finding my night's accommodation, the Tourist Information Centre around the corner from the pier. Finding a room isn't that easy so it's down the Esplanade to the Youth Hostel. The last time I stayed in a Youth Hostel I didn't have grey hair. Since then these hostels have also changed as evidenced by this room which is lovely, a good standard with four beds, toilet and shower. All the latest modern conveniences, and a swipe card door key which locks me out of the room with my kit inside. Shit. I hate modern technology!

A bed found for the night, thoughts now turn to my stomach. I meet a lovely lady in the kitchen who tells me about a veggie restaurant. I decide to give it a try. The meal, hommous, is only just O.K. but the Scottish heather beer certainly does the job. Now revitalised and less laden I call back at the Tourist Information Centre, to pick up a few leaflets, and whilst there I check out the current "Islands" book. As yet, no one has landed on all my islands. I wonder if I will land on them? Will I be the first? Is the first really important?

The beer and fresh air makes me realise that I am still hungry, so I set off to the local Tesco's for a staple diet of baked beans and chips. It starts to rain and I am thankful that I have brought my new jacket with me, as I head back to the Youth Hostel, from where I watch the sun re-appear and later set.

Listening to the conversations around me I realise how many people long to find their own quiet place, somewhere off the beaten track, away from other tourists. Oban is full of people. Business has been good for the tourist industry here over the last year and a half; although there is less overseas travel from the U.K. this hostel seems full of young Germans. Some of them seem full of life and others I sense are bored, just biding their time ready for their "real" life to begin. "Life is what happens whilst you are busy making other plans." said John Lennon.

The sunset is magnificent and I am at peace. I hope that Donald and the other boatmen will deliver me to the islands where I know my soul lies. These islands have a soul, individual and collective; it is only with their permission that I will land and leave; each one alive as you and I, each one a creation of the divine. I look out of the window over to Kerrera. It is just across the bay, so close that I can almost touch it. But for me it is too near, too busy. I am driven by the remoteness and isolation of uninhabited islands. This sunset is so beautiful; it would be a shame to miss it. I stroll outside. The air is fresh and I can feel my soul soar.

As the sun sets behind Kerrera the "Lord of the Isles" ferry sails majestically back into Oban Bay for the night. I am waiting, ready for my journey to begin.

After a fantastic night's sleep, I look out onto the Sound of Kerrera; it is exquisitely still, like a piece of fine silk. But this looks as though it will be the lull before the storm; the weather forecast predicts bad weather Sunday and Monday, and I begin to realise how much I will need God's support on my journey. I hope that you understand me when I say God. For me, "God" means that which is greater; "soul" to me means that which continues and "mind" I use to explain that of our thoughts.

I certainly need some divine intervention with my pack. It seriously needs reducing. This is my first test, how to reduce it in size yet not go hungry. Planning is not that easy when you really don't know when or where you will restock your food supply in the days ahead. Definitely a case of trial and error!

Not having the ability to even switch on a computer, nor possessing a mobile phone, I am reliant on phoning my home answer phone to see if Donald has been in touch. No message. I tell myself that the pace of life is different in the Western Isles. I hope.

Having arrived at the ferry terminal at 10.15am, excited as a child on Christmas morning, it promises to be a long wait as the Barra ferry doesn't leave until 2.50pm. Well at least I won't miss it! After a while, it's time for munchies, so I leave my kit at the ferry terminal and head for Tesco's.

Finally, it is time to go! I'm surprised that the Clansman ferry is much larger than I expected. But, before I even get on it, my backpack breaks. Not major, it's just where I put my jacket. Still I can manage, although I will need a new one for the next trip. The people on the ferry seem really friendly. They are on weekends away, whale watching, monitoring for a film, on motorbike trips. All sorts of people, on all kinds of journeys.

Sailing past Mull into open water I immediately forget about the problems with my backpack and focus on something I hadn't thought about before, my sea legs! Oh shit! Fortunately, diving porpoises and dolphins make a welcome distraction and before too long my islands appear. What a great sight! To have studied something for so long from the confines of my home, they are beyond my wildest imaginings. Berneray and Mingulay, majestically rising out of the water, look rocky, inhospitable, uninhabited and difficult to access. Reality hits home.

The ferry docks at Castlebay, Barra; island number one. O.K. it is the first, but not a "real island," for everyone comes here. The real islands are those beyond

Barra. To me Castlebay is another world; it is in a time warp of a world that never existed, and I love it. It is so small. I make my way to the hostel, which is welcoming and laid back. Just as I completely trusted the people on the ferry with my unattended bags, I am aware that this trust transports itself from the ferry to the island. It is a joy to experience.

I settle in at the hostel and give Donald's wife a phone call. She says that Donald will phone me late tomorrow morning at the hostel. There is a wedding on the island tonight and he will be a "wee bit hazy in the morning."

I do not sleep well. The wind and rain howl at my window all night. Is this a typical night, a bad night or heaven forbid a good night?!! Clyde, my travelling companion, a seven-inch brown teddy bear, is most concerned. I start to think that maybe I am crazy to even contemplate this adventure. Muldoanich looms across the bay, a steep unwelcoming island. Some of these islands you can almost touch from the shore, but getting to and from them will be quite a different story. I decide to brave the elements and go outside the front door. Yes, it is howling for sure, but once I'm out there it doesn't seem so bad. It certainly sounds a lot better. It seems that in my diverse life I have learnt many things and gained many skills; yet here in the Outer Hebrides the lesson that I have to learn is to wait. To wait for the weather, to wait for a phone call, to wait for Donald.

I had better explain. Donald Number One, the man with the boat on Barra, is currently overseas on holiday. I spoke to him before he left and he suggested that his friend, Donald Number Two to you and me, might be able to help in getting me out to my islands. So, this is the Donald that I am seeking. Not Donald Number One but Donald Number Two.

I wait in all morning by the hostel phone but, as you can guess, the call never comes. The pace of life here is so different from back home. I certainly would hate to be a diary salesman in this part of the world.

Eventually, around lunchtime, I decide to go outside and do some exploring. Armed with apple, peanuts, binoculars, camera and Clyde I walk to the Bagh Thalaman dunes. Here, I sit quietly on the seat overlooking the most breathtaking of locations. I feast my eyes on the rocks, the sheep in the distance, the powerful waves that hit the most perfect of soft sandy beaches. It surprises me that there are so few birds here. I wonder if it is because of the wind? After some time I take a slow walk to the local burial ground, set in such a raw environment it is proof that we humans are just a sideshow. The Celtic crosses in the graveyard fill me with a sense of wonder; they are beautiful, uplifting symbols guiding the soul, a link between earth and the world beyond.

As I leave to walk towards the dunes once more, I pass a parked car with its window open and the keys inside. Such trust amongst this community is a joy to all those who are fortunate enough to observe it.

I walk briskly back to the hostel, the cob webs well and truly blown away. I think I have walked five miles in total. Back at the hostel, I am greeted by the sight of an American, sporting an above average waistline; he is fast asleep in one of the armchairs. Snoring contentedly he reminds me of a beached whale. I decide that I am in need of sustenance and head for the local Co-op. I treat myself to a packet of "Hob Nobs," some vegan chocolate and some sensible food. An addiction to "Hob Nobs" may not be widely understood unless of course you happen to be a fellow addict. OK I know that they will make me fat and that an overdose of them will cause me to feel sluggish and sleepy, but before I fall asleep my addictive personality will be a joyous one. So forget the Atkins Diet I say and bring on the carbs!!

Still no call from Donald Number Two. I take solace in a moon that illuminates Kismul Castle, (which gave its name to Castlebay), after which I enjoy a party in the pub, before heading back to the hostel to sleep and dream of that elusive phone call.

I am up at 7.00am feeling bright and full of energy. The sky, a vivid orange, reminds me of "the shepherd's warning." I enjoy an "alternative breakfast" of boiled potatoes, carrots, ketchup, black pepper, "Hob Nobs" and coffee. My rationale in preparing such a culinary delight is that, when I do eventually leave, potatoes will be heavy and take time to cook, as well as using a lot of gas. But "Baked Beans" can wait. I don't believe it; now even my beans are waiting!

All this waiting. I decide to wait until 11.00am, and then go walkabout. If I don't get out onto my islands, I've got to accept that it's not right and there must be something better waiting for me elsewhere. I suppose at least, if I don't go today, I'll be able to touch base with Ruth who is returning tonight from her girl's weekend in Paris.

I feel heartened by my new plan. I will definitely leave Barra by Wednesday to who knows where, but in the meantime I'm going out! I decide to take a walk up to the North Bay which coincidentally passes Donald's house! As I get to the Catholic Church it starts to rain, so I take refuge inside. I should like to say that I spent my time there in prayer and meditation, but would be stretching the truth too far as, in time-honoured tradition, I fall asleep.

Feeling refreshed I continue my walk all the way to the ferry terminal, what a fantastic six to seven mile stroll it's been. Just as I approach the terminal I see the most beautiful rainbow arching over Fuday. This is too much! I can almost touch it, Fuday and four of the other islands. The weather is perfect. Donald where are you?

Deep in thought I take the bus back to Castlebay. But it is not easy to concentrate for long; the bus driver is stressing out with the island school children insisting they wear their seat belts. All this reminds me of my own school days and the school bus journeys back to my village. I can still hear old Bert saying "With all this noise I can't hear myself speak." Funny the things you remember.

On the drive back to Castlebay, Donald's house door is still open.

I am in need of some liquid refreshment and so decide to give the Castlebay Arms a quick inspection. One beer later, arriving back at the hostel I am given a message from Donald. He rang at 11.30am and is ready to sail. Aaggh!! Excitedly I ring his number but once again only chat to his wife. She'll get him to ring me. I continue to wait. Monday comes to a close.

It is now Tuesday and I cannot believe that this is only my fifth day away. How is Donald Number Two? Still no news.

Whilst eating my lunch I decide that it's not important to lose weight. Instead I'll happily settle on not gaining weight! All in all today is a lazy relaxing day, a good opportunity to take afternoon coffee on the terrace at the hostel and decide what I am going to do.

Why I started my island journey on Barra I'll never know. Naive beginnings maybe?

I decide on plan number two. If I travel from Barra via Eriskay, through South Uist, Benbecula, Grimsay, North Uist and Skye then I will arrive in Mallaig in one day, from there I will be able to visit the Small Isles.

2

THE SMALL ISLES

Having booked the first bus out of Castlebay the night before, I am the only passenger onboard. Despite my initial setback, I am not downhearted. I disembark at the ferry terminal for Eriskay, and wait, looking out across the water towards the very islands that have thwarted me from visiting them this time. I know that I will return. I feel them just as I feel my own soul. We will be re-united. Of that I am certain.

My journey to Eriskay is quite magical and I take much delight from the variety of birds who accompany the boat, some flying just overhead and others sailing close by on the waves. This morning there is only one car and myself onboard. The sea is a picture of calm and the islands that I pass seem mystical and inviting. Regretfully, with not a signpost in sight, I don't even know if these are my islands or not. It is bad enough saying goodbye to Barra but even sadder for me to say farewell to islands that I do not even know.

Soon I am landing on Eriskay. From here I travel by bus across the causeways which link Eriskay to South Uist, Benbecula, Grimsay and North Uist. Since their construction the five islands have now become one for the purpose of my journey. Another day I will revisit to spend a night.

My ferry for Skye leaves from Lochmaddy, to the north-east of North Uist. Here I am welcomed by my first swarm of midges. I am glad to get onto the boat and leave the welcoming committee for the other passengers. My fellow travellers seem different from those on Barra, more urban, of the mainland; giving you a quick once over but not keen to exchange a smile or a few words.

We dock at Uig which is towards the north of Skye. Here I am pleasantly surprised to come across an almost "veggie" restaurant. My stomach quietened, I climb onboard the bus to Portree. There are only six passengers, including myself and a local man who entertains us on his bagpipes. It adds a nice traditional quality to our journey.

I am struggling to hold onto that wonderful Barra feel. As the bus pulls into Portree, the capital of Skye, I feel myself recoiling. Once again, I am surrounded by "civilisation". Traffic, Hotels, Souvenir Shops and Tourists. Get me out of here! I jump on the first bus to Armadale and bid Portree a hasty goodbye.

My journey to Armadale for the Mallaig ferry is memorable. I am accompanied by an American who is reminiscent of Meat Loaf with a cigar. Can he talk?! I remind myself that one of the delights of this part of the world is the cross section of people you meet along the way! Fortunately, Meat Loaf clone hits it off with a group of Geordies and I am left to my thoughts.

As we travel over to Mallaig, the sea breeze helps me settle once more. Mallaig, some love it. Me? Well, if you are simply travelling in the direction of another ferry then that's brilliant, but if you are staying the night, then its' not quite so good. Tonight I am staying, so I check into the hostel. It's six beds to each mixed sex dormitory.

I awake at six a.m. showering and eating my breakfast long before my room mates have surfaced.

Today I am travelling to Eigg, which, along with Rum, Muck and Canna, form the "Small Isles." Eigg is owned by the Isle of Eigg Heritage Trust. The Trust took official ownership on 12 June 1997, a partnership between the islanders, the Scottish Wildlife Trust and the Highland Council.

I am glad to leave Mallaig and I spend my journey to Eigg chatting to a couple of ladies; one a Hungarian is also planning to camp on the island. As we approach the huge, distinguishable peak, An Sgurr, the exposed summit of the island becomes visible in the distance. We are advised by "Cal Mac" not to disembark unless we plan to stay on Eigg for a few days. Inclement weather is forecast and we may get stuck there, the ferry being unlikely to get in. As we are assimilating this information we notice a smaller vessel sailing out from Eigg to meet us. We are then transferred onto the bobbing boat in mid ocean. Not being the best of swimmers, I am more than relieved once this process is complete. Eigg, at great expense and subject to much debate and difference of opinion, is having a new pier built at Galmisdale; which once complete will ensure our unusual method of transfer becomes a thing of the past.

Having landed on my island number two, it takes no time to get on to more practical matters and before we know it, we have spoken to the right person and settled our camping dues. As a Yorkshireman I am most impressed, only

£12 for me to camp there for four nights! My newly found friend and I walk to the campsite. What a wonderful location. There is a stream to the side of it, trees behind and, in front, a bay where the new pier is under construction. As far as my eye can see, are herons, oystercatchers and birds that I have never seen before.

Tents erected, we decide to take a walk together but manage to get totally lost and wet so, upon finding out that the tea room sells beer, we call in to meet the locals. The night is typically Hebridean with plenty of whisky and beer enjoyed in a cigarette-filled room.

I find myself well and truly pissed which makes it all the more difficult to understand what everyone is talking about. On Barra, when I didn't understand them I just put it down to the Gaelic. Here, on Eigg, I don't understand and they are talking English! It's all good banter and I enjoy sharing in the laughter as they recall tales from their day to day lives.

Eventually tiredness and common sense prevail and I decide to call it a day. I enjoy the slow walk back to my tent, past the jetty. It is 1.00am and a digger is still at work on the new pier. I don't watch too long, keen to sleep and to enjoy the experience of my first night under cover in my brand new tent.

After a good night's sleep, I awake refreshed and ready to head for pastures new. I bid "farewell" to my fellow camper and leave for Kildonnan Bay, taking the short cut over Eigg football pitch onto the cliff tops. It is not as easy as I have been assured it would be, particularly when I have to climb down a rock face and clamber over many boulders. But in the end my efforts are well rewarded and, when I finally get there, I am treated to a vast array of birds, and a colony of seals, basking in the sun. It is the first time I have come across seals and I feel so privileged to be able to watch them in their natural habitat.

As I continue my walk around the bay I come across a small black roofed wheel house, just the size of a bothy and made from stone, it is nestling amongst the hillside, which surrounds the bay. I stop to take a photograph of it before continuing on my journey. Next, I arrive at a ruined church where the gravestone of a McCallum catches my eye. The lady died young and her epitaph reminds me of Ruth's Aunty Lorna who has the same name.

Still feeling energetic, I decide to continue my walk towards the Grulin's on the southern coastline of Eigg, from where it is possible to see the islands of Muck and Rum. This takes me through two abandoned villages. At the first village I stop and sit on the top of a large boulder looking out onto the cliffs. Marvelling at the beautiful scenery and the feeling of complete peace which surrounds me, I think to myself "This is it, it doesn't get any better".

I pass a small bothy further along this path. How bleak and isolated it must be living up here in winter. I am walking along a track, not a road, so everything needed has to be carried here. Before long, I reach the second abandoned village, which is probably more beautiful than the first. The views from it are not as good as from the first village, although I can still make out Rum covered in mist in the distance.

It has been a good day. I feel as though I have really achieved something today. I guess that I must have covered nine to ten miles on my walk and although I am not exactly a paratrooper, realistically on a good day, more of a stroller, today's excursion has been a considerable exercise for me, and I can't wait to tell Ruth all about it.

Back at my tent, I write up my journal, wash the pans from my evening meal in the stream, and button down the hatches. Tonight will be the first time that I have spent the whole evening in the darkness of my tent, there being no "Bar Night" tonight on the island. It certainly sounds windy outside and I hope that my new tent is strong enough to cope. It has been a wonderful day, energetic and fulfilling.

I awake, having slept OK, although I seem to have misplaced my ear plugs somewhere. The tent has lasted the night and I am still in one piece.

Tonight, being Saturday, it is one of the two "Bar Nights" in the tea room on Eigg. About 9.30am I finally surface from my tent. It is cold and I have had to put on my thermal trousers and a third top. I head up to the "centre," to give my teeth a clean in the toilet / shower area. The centre comprises a restaurant cum bar, grocery shop, souvenir and information centre, toilets with shower facilities, a storage room and entrance area with useful information for visitors and islanders alike. Before leaving, whilst in conversation with one of the islanders, I learn that there are three bothys to rent on the island for about £125 a week. Maybe next time.

I set off to walk over to some caves. I have been told that they are worth a visit and so I leave in a south-westerly direction from Galmisdale. It is a really pleasant walk if a little steep, dropping down about 100 metres to get to them. I surprise myself when I find the walk back afterwards not too difficult. Both the caves have significant history attached to them. The smaller of the two "Massacre Cave," got its name in 1577 when 395 MacDonalds, hiding from a Macleod raid, suffocated in it as their enemies tried to smoke them out. The second, its sister, Cathedral Cave, is the larger of the two in size, but not length. It has less to distinguish itself, apart from offering refuge to a decapitated dead swan.

All this walking is hot work and so I remove my waterproof trousers and third top before making the return journey. On the way back, I am aware that my walking ability is improving. When I arrive back at the shop, someone asks me if I am working on the new pier. It's a small island and so my new face is quickly noticed. Purely to be sociable, I stop for a beer or two before returning to my tent for a siesta.

Feeling fully refreshed, I return to the tea room. It's a quiet evening and I begin to realise how much of an insular society is Eigg. Maybe all islands are insular? At the moment I am in the company of some of the workers from the pier project, but once their work is completed, I know that this tea room will become very quiet. After reading all the notices on display and listening to various snippets of conversation, I decide that Eigg is like a Gandhi Ashram. It feels like a place for social experimentation. By that, I mean that through their recent ownership of this island, and all the democratic processes that have been created, it has resulted in a lot of meetings for the islanders.

Once again, I stumble back to my tent pissed! Two out of three nights in such a state. Tonight is the worst yet and I end up falling over my tent in the dark. At least this proves that my tent is strong enough to withstand all eventualities.

As Sunday, is my last full day on the island, I intend to make the most of it. Inspired by my earlier improvement on the walking front, I decide to rise early and make the eight mile round trip to Cleadale, at the north-west of the island.

I am amazed to arrive at the village quite so quickly. My first sight of it, with Rum in the background, completely takes my breath away. Wow! It is magnificent, like visiting another world. Cleadale is so different from the rest of Eigg, with its large expanse of flat grazing land and steep hills behind. Nestling amongst the greenery, protected by the hills and looking out towards the sea, are about 15 houses, where most of the islanders live. I leave the islanders to their solitude and wander northwards, in search of my own, towards the hills of Blar Mor.

It is a beautiful day, bright blue skies with little cloud. I am so lucky with the weather. My walk towards Blar Mor takes me past a green and white caravan, enclosed inside its own walled garden complete with garden seat and private stream. Island sheep scatter as I walk past. As the terrain starts to get steeper I begin to breathe more deeply. I am glad that I didn't attempt this on day one, I certainly would have struggled. Without doubt, I am going to be much fitter by the time I get home.

The strenuous steep walk is well worth the effort and I am able to rest for a while admiring Rum and its Cuillins just across the water. Down below me in the distance, I watch two small children and their parents making sandcastles on yet another fabulous, deserted beach. They do so in blissful ignorance of my observations from up above. As I continue my walk along the cliffs I feel so serene, surrounded by all this beauty, which seems never ending. Far below me, only hills and rocks and sea. Here, in this elevated position, I feel about as near to perfection as I could ever wish to be. I take Clyde out of my pocket and place him amongst the soft grass. He looks so small sitting there, almost disappearing amongst the blades of grass; he seems to be shouting out to me "Don't let me fall!" I take his picture and continue my walk.

It takes me up to a deserted Catholic Church. No wonder it's deserted, surely only the sheep would have made it up here. As I go inside, I notice a solitary candle burning brightly and realise that someone else has been here before me today. The walls might be cracked and the plaster breaking away, but within this church there is such a feeling of love and devotion.

As I make my way back to Galmisdale, I am feeling quite elated. It has been a wonderful walk and my own walking ability has been a major plus. My mind is stable and my phone contact with Ruth has been perfect.

After a drink in the tea room, I know that my time on Eigg is complete. Although I haven't climbed An Sgurr, I am happy with what I have seen and done here. Eigg has not been what I expected but, because my experience of Scottish islands is so limited, I really didn't expect anything in the first place! Eigg is different from anything I've ever experienced before, it is a social experiment and one day I'd love to visit it again.

I make my way back to my tent. As I sit there, writing up my journal and enjoying a cup of coffee, a group of tourists from the Hebridean Princess cruise liner walk past. Because of their lack of appropriate clothing, they are struggling to cross the stream. I think to myself that I wouldn't change places with them for all the riches in the world. To me, to experience the beauty of nature in its rawest form, will always be far more satisfying than any pleasures I could gain from travelling in such luxury.

It is now Monday morning, and the day I say goodbye to Eigg. I treat myself to a shower and hair wash, my first since Mallaig. With my long hair, it is always a challenge, getting it washed and dried, away from home. But, today, I even manage to blow dry it! Here on Eigg there is an honesty box at "the centre" for use of the shower. I really like this idea, which surely encourages and brings out the best in people. I put in extra for the electric I have used.

Sweden has rejected the Euro today. Nice one. I pack all my gear away and take down my tent for the first time. Having cooked some food my backpack, thankfully, is slightly lighter than before.

Now, all I have to do is wait for the ferry. I treat myself to a coffee and vegan flapjack at the tea room. I sit watching as all the pier construction workers call in for their traditional breakfasts of sausage, bacon, eggs, black pudding, white toast and milky tea. Not for me, but each to their own.

As we leave Eigg on the transfer boat, all the cargo has to be lifted from it over our heads onto the ferry. I wonder what health and safety would make of it all?

It took me a long time to realise that Eigg possessed such a wonderful mix of humanity amongst its many hidden treasures. I would have to visit many more islands to truly appreciate the beauty of Eigg and the delightful diversity of its people. Without doubt, Eigg is a gem of an island.

Leaving Eigg the ferry makes the short crossing to Rum; island number three. Rum is the largest of the Small Isles group but, because of its mountainous terrain and inhospitable climate only about 30 people live there. Since 1957 this island has been owned by Scottish Natural Heritage.

We dock at the pier on Loch Scresort, which is to the east of the island. I am not arriving here alone. Today, many older visitors are also visiting. I guess that most of them are around retirement age. Unlike me, they are not camping, choosing instead to book into Kinloch Castle, with its dormitory accommodation.

To me, Rum has an unusual feel with its diverse mix of people. It consists of a combination of older tourists drawn by the castle, outdoor types attracted by the Cuillins and Rum's varied wildlife, and Scottish Natural Heritage (SNH) volunteers and employees. Because of such a transient population, Rum does not possess the sense of community that Eigg has.

I set up camp in what must be "midge" capital of the world and afterwards take a stroll towards the other side of the bay. It is warm and comfortable so I decide to sunbathe. But, before I realise it I have fallen asleep and wake up feeling groggy and in need of some food!

Back at camp, I start cooking. This is not as easy as it sounds. Sporting the latest fashion in designer midge nets, over my head, I eventually manage to rustle something up, escaping to eat it inside my tent, to avoid any further bites. These midges have certainly had a field day chomping away on my hands and wrists.

After my tea, I visit the General Store, which also serves as the unofficial Pub on the island. Having visited Rum once before, I know that it is run as a co-operative and that everyone volunteers their time freely to keep it running. I immediately recognise a couple of the locals from my last visit. Having successfully integrated into island life on Rum they are definitely a credit to the place. Once more, in time honoured fashion, I end up drunk.

I ask myself, what sort of journey is this? Is it a journey to the 162 islands of Scotland, a spiritual journey or is it just a piss up? I guess a combination of all three but, so far, it has become strongly alcohol-biased!

On the way back home from the "pub", I call Ruth from a phone box which has no door. Well, it does, only it's lying some thirty feet away. I don't know why I should give the matter a second thought, apart from the sea birds, there's no one else around here to listen to our conversation. Afterwards, as I wander slowly back towards the tent, I see the red globe of Mars shimmering ahead of me so clearly in the sky. At the moment it is as near to us on Earth as it has been in almost 60,000 years. What an absolutely perfect night. Once again, safely back at my tent, I look over towards the moon, which is at the other side of the bay. It is only just over half its normal size, but its light still manages to illuminate the whole bay. Before I know it, I have fallen asleep.

Today I intend walking to Kilmory Bay. It is at the north of the island, a 13 mile round trip; which will be my furthest walk yet. My walking stick is definitely proving to be a great asset; it means that I am able to walk much further through all sorts of terrain. I make good time and before I know it, I have reached Kilmory itself, where I discover a laundry shed. It is the place where, in bygone days, the Laird of Kinloch Castle used to send his sheets and smalls to be washed, deeming it entirely inappropriate to air his dirty washing in view of his own castle!

As I start to leave the sands of Kilmory Bay and head back across the moors to Kinloch, I catch sight of a stag in the distance; his antlers silhouetted against the rocks. Am I down wind of him? I'm not sure. Gradually, bit by bit, I edge closer, trying not to startle him. He is definitely aware of me. Finally, I get within six metres and take a series of photos. What a magnificent, powerful beast he is, with the most beautiful strong brown eyes. At this distance, his antlers look particularly menacing and sharp. Majestically he stares straight into my eyes. I try to breathe calmly, hoping he won't sense my heart racing and brain screaming "Get running!" Not being the best of runners my feet are glued to the spot. As I stand, transfixed, I notice he is wearing a collar. Eventually, after what seems like an eternity, this magnificent Stag decides I am not worthy of any more of his time and wanders off swiftly in search of his next engagement.

What a thrill! I am exhilarated by this experience and walk all the way back to the campsite like a paratrooper, well almost! The round trip has only taken me just over three hours walking time and I am feeling really pleased with myself. On Rum, when you go walkabout, you are asked to complete a form, detailing your probable route and the walk start and anticipated end time. This means that should you fail to return, the Scottish Natural Heritage (S.N.H.) can come looking for you; but also they can identify the most popular walks on the island for their own future plans. Personally, I feel it's more like 1984, but I go along with it all and sign in and out.

Back at camp, the midges are still as bad as last night, so I am forced to cook my food on my little gas stove inside the tent.

My stomach full once more, I decide that it is time for a little social interaction. I opt for another night in the general store. Once there, I find myself perched on one of the two stools. An added benefit of this arrangement is that whilst you are contemplating life from the comfort of your stool, you generally remember some odd bits of shopping that you need!

Eventually the last few tourists leave and I am left on my stool, observing the other "shoppers" in the store. I guess that their ages are between 25 and 45 years old. The one common denominator, the bond that seems to tie them together, is the S.N.H. the main employer on the island. The bulk of their conversation is about their love hate relationship with the S.N.H. I question the love bit.

After two days on Rum it is now time to leave. I am pleased about this. For although Rum has some lovely individuals, I do question if a true community really exists here.

The ferry ride to Canna, island number four, seems a bit choppy for this time of year. I arrive there, accompanied by several other ferry passengers who are visiting the island on a day trip from Mallaig. They will spend just an hour and a half here.

Canna, the most westerly of the Small Isles, is owned by the National Trust for Scotland. It is bigger in size than Muck but smaller than Rum and Eigg. Only 14 people live here. It is about five and a half miles long, a mile and a half wide and is connected to Sanday, by a footbridge, at its south-easterly extremity. The pier where our ferry has docked is actually in the natural harbour between Canna and Sanday.

After some confusion, during which I search for a non-existent bunkhouse, finally I am directed towards the side of the church where I set up camp. I am feeling great. O.K., so it's very windy and starting to rain, but I'm alive and doing something that I know most people could never do. I am 38 years old. Yet in many ways I have still managed to retain my youthful exuberance, feeling equally at home chilling out in a tent with no shower or enjoying the five-star experience of a nice hotel, theatre trip and strutting my stuff in a suit and tie.

Once my tent is erected, I decide to try out the harbour tearoom. I am in luck. It is open for a couple of hours on Wednesday afternoons and as well as serving lunches it is fully licensed. You've guessed, I opt for a beer!

I spend the rest of the afternoon in the bay area, just strolling and stopping to rest or talk to passing visitors and generally take in the wonderful fresh air. There is so much to observe here, seals, oystercatchers, herons and other sea birds; all of them completely at home amongst the fishing boats and yachts that slip in and out of Canna Harbour throughout the year.

There are two churches on Canna; Saint Columba's Presbyterian Church and Saint Columba's Roman Catholic Chapel. I am camping behind the Presbyterian Church, easily distinguishable by its rocket shaped bell tower. Inside the church, facing each other are some wooden pews and to the left of the entrance is the bell tower. Although there is no electricity or heating here, I know that I will be glad to take advantage of this peaceful place to sit quietly each day and write my journal. However, the Roman Catholic Chapel, which is near to the farm, is the one the islanders use the most. It has been beautifully restored so that it can be used as a place of worship for the small island community. I love the austere, traditional feel of these Scottish churches and believe that Gandhi would have approved of them too. It has taken much investment from many interested parties in recent times, to maintain the history and the heritage of these islands and to ensure that their treasures will remain for the benefit of residents and visitors alike for many years to come.

As the evening starts to draw in, I enjoy a glass of beer. I am the only customer in the tea room and as I don't want to outstay my welcome I bid the proprietor "Goodnight." The hospitality here has been the most welcoming of all the Small Isles so far, even allowing me to use their toilet when the shop is closed. Such kindness and consideration.

At the pier, a graffiti covered rock face, daubed in every colour and style imaginable cannot fail to intrigue visitors to Canna. On it are the names of many of the fishing boats, which have anchored here in bygone years, their inscriptions now fading under the newer, brighter names of the more recent island visitors who also yearn to be immortalised. It certainly catches your eye as you enter the beautiful harbour.

It is now 9.30am and having enjoyed another good night's sleep, I am raring to go. Today I have chosen a ten mile walk, which will take me along the south coast of the island and back. The early part of the walk is easy enough along a farm track and then over grassland, which, although undulating, is reasonable. However, the terrain soon starts to change as the hills become steeper and rockier. Before long, I have reached Tarbert Bay with its dramatic basalt columns of rock. In the distance, about five miles away, I can see the Hyskeir lighthouse.

Reaching the south-westerly end of the island, I am bowled over. From my lofty position, I gaze out onto a tiny cluster of islands, bathed in the most beautiful azure sea. I feel as though I am looking out on the Tropics, not the Hebrides. I sit transfixed as colonies of seabirds swoop down to collect their lunch, framed in this magnificent picture postcard scene.

As I continue my walk along the west coast of Canna, I am feeling quite elated. Unfortunately, this mood does not last long. Suddenly the skies open, the rain pours down and, before I realise it, I have walked into a bog! The end result is that both my feet and boots are soaked, in spite of having sprayed my boots before leaving home. I promise myself that, as soon as I get back to Yorkshire, I will invest in a decent pair of waterproof boots.

Squelching with each step, I search in vain for some underground dwellings, which I have been assured are somewhere up here. But, in the end, I give in; after all if they are underground how the hell am I meant to see them anyway?

Reaching the top of yet another hill, the mist suddenly descends and my visibility is dramatically reduced. I freeze, wondering what to do next. Then, as quickly as it appeared, the mist rises and I am extremely relieved to see my route ahead once more.

I am pleased to make good use of the first toilet I come across, to clean my teeth, shave, and brush my hair. Feeling much more human, I walk back towards my tent and inevitably, my thoughts turn to the possibility of a beer. The tea room is open Monday to Saturday from 6pm to 11pm but with so few tourists about, I wonder whether it will be open this evening?

It is great to be back at my tent, my home. My first task is to remove my boots and wring out the water from my socks. My cold, damp feet remind me of two white wrinkled prunes. I spend the next half an hour, ably assisted by my Swiss Army knife, cutting off horrible softened toe nails. I love my knife, although when I tried unsuccessfully to use its tin opener gadget the other night, I ended up leaving a gouge on the handle, a reminder of my endeavours.

The news is not good. The tea room does not look as though it is going to open tonight. I keep popping my head out of the tent to see any signs of life, but the shop door remains firmly closed. I try to manage my disappointment by telling myself I am drinking far too much anyway, and that if the tea room doors remain closed, it has got to be a good thing. I grunt to myself in acknowledgment of this staggering home truth. For all true Yorkshiremen grunting is already second nature, but I am beginning to notice that, in this part of the world, grunting is also a most advanced form of communication.

Here, many people have trouble with the different Scottish accents, but more people seem to have trouble understanding me. I am told that I speak fast. I don't speak fast, they listen slowly!

I enjoy a good meal, listen to my radio and then it is time to sleep. By 8.30 pm, I am surrounded by darkness and the sound of the wind.

This is my last day on Canna. I am up and out of my tent by 8.30 am. I've had a good ten hours sleep and am feeling relaxed and rejuvenated.

I try and call Ruth, but the phone box doesn't seem to be working properly. I can hear her but she can't hear me; even though the phone has gobbled my money up. My socks are still wet and so are my boots; I have run out of coffee and the weather is wet and windy. Back home you'd say it was a shit day, yet here, hey no worries. Ruth will know that it was me trying to get through. I'll not wear my socks. The coffee – ah, well. The weather? I'm sure I saw the sun for a few minutes!

Here in my little tent, I am more in tune with the elements than I could ever be in a smart hotel and yes, at this exact moment, I would definitely appreciate such comforts. But after two or three days I know it would do me in. Being at one with nature may reduce creature comforts, but you are compensated a hundred fold by the joy your soul experiences when it is free.

Perhaps on Muck I'll find a bunkhouse where I can get my underwear and maybe my jeans washed. It would also be great to wash my hair and have a shower. Although these things sound inviting, and I look forward to the prospect of them, I am also aware that, for me, a trade off will ultimately be the loss of my soul connection. Living in a tent in these conditions has brought me so close to nature. Having said all that, I have gone five whole days without a shower and nine days since I slept in a bed!

My walk today is to Canna's neighbouring island, Sanday. Linked by a footbridge and, except at high tide, sandbanks, Sanday is to the south-west of Canna, separated only by a narrow tidal channel. The footbridge reminds me of a bridge I once crossed in Rishikesh, in the foothills of the Indian Himalayas. It was busy with people going about their daily business. This one, in contrast is completely deserted, there is not a soul about. I enjoy my walk across and feel quite safe in the process. From time to time, I glance over my shoulder at Canna. It strikes me just how unpopulated the island is, with only a few houses scattered about.

Having reached the other side, I sit on a rock and rest watching a colony of seals, lazing about on a small crop of rocks in the Boat Harbour. I guess I'm only 50 feet away from them but, as I rise to try to get closer, they drop into the water out of sight. I'm dismayed to think that I have frightened them. But, after only a few minutes, they reappear, their heads bobbing out of the sea, looking like submarine telescopes rising up from the deep. I'm thrilled to learn that they are most inquisitive of creatures and that, from the safety of the water, they are quite happy to draw closer and give me the once over! Finally, I fail to hold their attention any longer and they leave me, swimming back over to their rocks, where they appear to go to sleep.

I stroll back towards the tea room and the sun appears. It is so nice to see it again. Relaxing outside on a chair, as a Calmac ferry sails into view, I would swear I was in the Mediterranean. I'm so lucky to be enjoying yet another idyllic picture postcard scene. I enjoy some banter with two guys who have just come off the boat, before they set off up the hills to stretch their legs.

I decide to give Ruth another call and this time we manage to hear each other O.K. She is working in London and says that from her window she is looking out towards the Houses of Parliament and the River Thames. In the background, I can actually hear the noise of a police car siren. I ask her to listen for a moment, and as she does I hold the receiver out of the phone box into the fresh air. After a few moments I return it to my ear and ask "Can you hear that?" "What?" she asks. "Precisely." It makes me realise how quiet my life is up here on the Small Isles. Apparently, today London is enjoying 25 degrees of sunshine. Here on Canna, it is about 15 degrees and, although it has been wet and windy for the past week, I'm not bothered. I wouldn't swap what I have for anything. The less you have the more you are grateful for. I say "Good night" to Ruth and stroll back to the tea room.

Tonight the tea room is open for the evening, which is good news. Joining me are four guys, who have moored in the bay with their yacht, and three contractors who are involved in rock drilling for the new pier.

Unfortunately, inside we learn some bad news. A local man has drowned off Muck whilst out with his lobster pots. Wendy the owner of the tea room suggests that I don't visit tomorrow as planned, as all of the islanders will be occupied in other ways. Muck has a population of around 30 people, about twice that of Canna. I take on board Wendy's advice and agree that now is not the right time to visit.

I decide on plan number three. If I travel back to Mallaig and catch a train to Oban, from there I can visit Mull, Iona and Ulva.

3
ON THE TOURIST TRAIL

SATURDAY 20TH SEPTEMBER 2003
TO FRIDAY 26TH SEPTEMBER 2003

The Mallaig ferry leaves at 8.30am and I am awake early, my thoughts still occupied with last night's news. Once my bags are packed, I make use of the church floor to roll up my tent; I do feel that God will approve of one of his houses being used to assist this traveller on his way.

Visiting Rum, then Eigg, the ferry maps the route that I have already taken. As I bathe in the sea breeze, the birds calling above me, I look out towards Eigg and reflect how much has happened since I arrived there only ten days before. Today we have arrived early and will have to wait for the transfer boat to connect with us.

As we finally leave its coastline for deeper waters, I look and see Muck in the distance. The man who drowned has still not been found.

Back on Mallaig's shores, I head straight for the Backpacker's Hostel. I cannot wait to get clean! I stand for ages in the shower so relieved to finally be able to wash my hair. Going native certainly does make you appreciate the simpler things in life. I am still itching from the Rum midges, the little bastard's. Hung over from last night it's certainly not true what the Scots believe about Irn-Bru. Three cans and I'm feeling like death. I decide that maybe it's time to give the drink a break.

After a brief catnap, I am feeling a bit better and take a stroll into town to do some shopping, buy a paper, eat and check out the train times for Oban. Now that I am clean, fed and enjoying a decent newspaper, I feel civilised again. I also feel that perhaps I have been a wee bit hasty about Mallaig. As I watch the sun shining over the fishing boats, I realise that it is a lovely place, especially around the harbour.

I dry out my tent and sort out my pack. Today it is time for readjustment, to be surrounded by people once again. I am feeling good, although I do recognise that I have become quieter, more settled. I love nature and the feeling of isolation. I also love going walkabout. I guess that I've grown out of the "long haul scene" and being surrounded by the Costa del Sol brigade. Having travelled for so many years through India, Thailand etc. I've heard it all before. Yet, around these islands I am meeting individuals at every turn, people who have original thoughts and I love it.

I am so fortunate to be so well travelled and to live such a simple life. "Simple living – high thinking." said M.K. Gandhi.

Keen to get onto my next adventure, I check out of the hostel a little too early and end up having to wait an hour and a half before my train leaves for Oban.

This journey has to be one of the most breathtaking in Scotland. What a wealth of beauty. I look out of my train window onto nature at its very best. Lochs as blue as fields of cornflowers; a young red doe shocked by our early morning intrusion; fast flowing rivers crashing over rocks; trees unbelievably sprouting from rocks; more beauty than the naked eye could possibly behold. As the train swings me round each horseshoe bend, I gaze incredulously as every picture becomes more amazing than the one before.

I am so rapt in the beauty of it all, that we reach Crianlarich before I realise. What a lovely little station; it reminds me of Darjeeling in India. My connecting train soon arrives and I enjoy my journey south.

Back in Oban once more, I check into the Youth Hostel and head for town in search of some food! I've been looking forward to a Chinese meal for a few days now. What a shame I got so excited. The chips are oily, the rice average and the mushroom and vegetable curry tasteless. The only good part of the meal is the Chinese tea. It's been a long time since I've had such a bad meal and I leave without giving a tip. The only tip for this place is don't visit it.

By sitting back in the chair and writing up my journal, I manage to avoid a heated debate at the hostel, about Tony Blair. After reading my book for a while, I decide to call it a night. Tomorrow I am going to Mull and from there, Ulva. It's been two days since I touched any alcohol.

I am on the 10am ferry from Oban to Craignure, Mull, the largest island of the Inner Hebrides. It is 50 miles from North to South and houses a population of just under 3000 people. Tobermory, the main centre on the island, appears on many picture postcards with its multi coloured houses.

I jump straight off the ferry and catch the Craignure bus on its way to Tobermory. I am going to get off at Salen, about ten miles away. From here, I plan to cross Mull at its narrowest point, only three miles wide, and make my way to the Ulva ferry. This all seems straightforward. However, after unsuccessfully sticking my thumb out for some time at Salen junction, I start to walk. The scenery begins to change as the forests give way to peat moors and I can see little sign of life, apart from the odd isolated farm. My initial optimism is starting to fade, even allowing for my recent fitness, carrying 30kg of kit for three miles in the pouring rain is no fun.

Feeling shattered, I eventually reach the other side of the island, at the junction of the road to Ulva. Once again, I try my luck at hitchhiking and this time I am successful. After only ten minutes, a lovely lady stops to give me a lift. We share a most enjoyable journey, talking of life on Mull and about two ladies, who wanted to spend a week on Eorsa for charity, but had to be taken off, after they became frightened of the strong winds. Eorsa is one of the islands that I will eventually visit. I'm not intimidated by this story; I have every confidence in my tent.

Soon I am at Ulva pier and slide the wooden window across to red to let the boatman know that I need a lift. As we sail across, I ask him if he knows of any boatman who might be able to take me out to Eorsa and Inch Kenneth, but he doesn't. I am trying wherever possible to build up my contacts, yet all these uninhabited islands seem difficult to access.

It is only a short crossing so within five minutes I am on Ulva; island number five.

I spot a small boathouse café close by, this is where I must pay for the boat crossing and discuss my camping arrangements. The telephone box here can only be used for emergencies. Ah well, at least it's being put to good use as a small greenhouse to grow someone's tomatoes in!

I set off to walk the three miles along the north side of the island towards Gometra. The last mile of my journey is absolutely exhausting and I am well and truly knackered by the time I eventually get there. I erect my tent but realise that I am on too steep a slope. There is nothing for it but to move camp and, if I thought that I was knackered before, then now I am feeling even worse! It's 7.10pm and dusk is closing in fast. Hurriedly I get most of my possessions outside the tent and remove the pegs from the ground. The wind is getting up and I'm really struggling to get my tent pegged back down amongst all this heather. Suddenly, a strong gust of wind catches the tent and I am left hanging onto it for dear life. I feel like a parachutist before he comes into land and know, that if I let go, I shall see the last of my tent before it flies off towards Mull. Using every last ounce of strength I finally pin it to the ground, after which I quickly move my kit to the safety of camp number two. Phew!

I lie in my tent and listen to the wind howling outside and before I know it my exhausted body is asleep.

I awake marvelling at the design of my tent. What a robust piece of equipment it is. Last night the wind and rain was terrible, and many times, I lay awake thinking that any moment my tent would take off towards the mainland with me hanging onto it. I don't think that I was frightened, but I was definitely concerned, shall we say.

Eventually about 11am, the wind drops and finally I am confident that my tent is no longer going to blow away. I decide to explore Gometra further. It is connected to Ulva by a causeway crossing Am Bru, a narrow tidal channel. Gometra is a beautiful place abundant with all kinds of wildlife. As I wander around, enjoying the freedom of a day with no rigid plans, I come across timid sheep, herons and a stag, which runs across the heather in front of me, and disappears as quickly as it appeared.

Just as I am returning to my tent, I notice a colony of seals in Am Bru. I decide to stop and watch them for a while and, before very long, realise that they are also watching me. Quite interested to gauge their reaction, I start to sing and am really surprised when they start swimming closer and closer towards where I am standing on the hill. They are without doubt the first audience ever to enjoy my singing!

Later, as I lie in my tent listening to Radio Scotland, I hear a strange noise. I peer outside and notice that the water level is rising in the tidal channel between Gometra and Ulva. Staring hard, I'm particularly drawn to a couple of large circles in the water, close to where the causeway connects the two pieces of land. To me, the circles look as though they are getting wider and wider. Wondering if they are two divers, I dig out my binoculars to take a closer look. I can't believe my eyes. Two seals have swum along the causeway, to a point in the water directly below my tent, and are making an almighty racket. It is as though they've come to invite me to play out with them! When they realise that I've seen them, they look up as if to say "Good night" before they swim away. I'm sure that they knew I was up there on the hill in my tent. So, I reach the end of my first full day spent in total isolation. Not one person or mobile phone to spoil the peace. It is an amazing feeling.

I awake after a quieter night's sleep. There has been a lot less wind. It's time to move on again, but I'm not sure where to.

On my way back I meet a four wheel drive vehicle delivering a satellite dish to one of the properties on Gometra. The driver has got over to Ulva using a barge pulled by a boat. Further along my way, I meet another vehicle with fish boxes on the back. This morning it's like the rush hour here! The driver asks me if I am the one who has been camping and seems amazed to learn that I have been out in my tent the night before last, during the bad weather.

Mentally and physically the three mile walk back to the Ulva ferry along the seriously potholed track really gets to me. I am absolutely exhausted as I climb up and down the banks at either side of the track, trying to avoid the massive puddles, which fill the potholes, as well as having to carry my 30kg backpack. For me, the most important part of my journey is to keep my head right and now I recognise that it is time to head for home. Tonight I will stay on Iona, then tomorrow night in Oban. Having made this decision my load starts to feel a lot lighter and I have more of a spring in my step. My trip has definitely not gone according to plan and now is the time to go home and do some re-thinking.

After four days without any alcohol I decide to treat myself to two small bottles of Becks at the boathouse café. Whilst they are nice they are not nearly as good as my expectation of them. My taste buds once more satisfied, I call the ferryman to take me back across to Mull.

In only a few minutes I am back over the water and waiting at the top of the road for some transport. I wait and I wait. Eventually, just as I am starting to give up hope of ever moving from this spot, the Post Bus, a red estate car, pulls up and gives me a lift all the way to Salen. Great! But, at Salen I am forced to wait and wait again. It is over three hours until the next bus arrives, so there is nothing for it but to stick out my thumb once more. Three hitches and some three hours later, I finally reach Fionnphort. This is where I catch the ferry to Iona.

Being only a short distance from the Mull coastline, my ferry journey to Iona, island number six, does not take long. Iona is famous as the place where, in 563 AD Columba landed and founded a monastery, which today draws 500,000 visitors a year to the island.

But this particular visitor is not in search of the Abbey. I am looking forward to some comfort for the night. It is not as straightforward as I had hoped the first B&B is full and there is no answer at the second. So I walk to the hostel which is about a mile away, to the north of the island.

The hostel is modern, its rooms spacious and clean with perfect shower rooms. There's a dining kitchen / lounge area which is large and comfortable. But, in spite of all these comforts, I don't like the place. It feels strange, yet no one agrees with me, when I mention it to a few of the other people staying here. Then I realise why. It is not the hostel, it is me. Having spent so much time on my own of late, I am feeling unsettled being surrounded by people and a few creature comforts once again.

I sit and talk a little; I enjoy the simple pleasures of a shower, shave and hair wash, play a game of chess, then eat. Now I am beginning to feel much better and more able to enjoy this beautiful island for what it is. It has been such a strange time readjusting from the isolation of Ulva to sharing my life with other people once more. I wonder how I will cope returning to Oban, "the big city" tomorrow?

It's 9am and I am watching the Mull coastline draw nearer. It is a very rough crossing for September, yet I like the feeling of the boat bouncing up and down and the wind blowing through my hair. One day, I hope Ruth and I will come back to Iona.

Safely back on dry land, I am left alone to enjoy my thoughts and the spectacular scenery as the Craignure bus twists and twines along the single track road through the Ross of Mull. Although Mull is too big for me, I cannot fail to be impressed by its stunning views.

I will return to Mull some other time and spend a night there. Now I am starting to get that "home again" feeling as I board the Oban ferry, clutching my newspaper. Soon I am sailing past Kerrera and Oban Bay is opening up before me. I know that my emotions are all over the place, my head is taking me home but my soul is still trying to catch me up. I am in need of some serious readjusting.

The open doors of St. Columba's Cathedral, on the Esplanade, offer me the refuge that I am seeking. I light a candle and watch it burn brightly from my seat. For the first time today I begin to feel peaceful. Oban and Mallaig have been perfect bases for me. They offer the traveller a half way house, only a breath away from both the world of nature and the hustle and bustle of urban civilisation.

After another good night's sleep at the Youth Hostel it is finally time to go home to Yorkshire.

The morning sky is as beautiful as my first sunset in Oban, only three weeks before. So much has happened to me in that time and I know that I am a very different person returning to York. I say goodbye to Oban.

York's Victorian Station seems cold and unwelcoming. I walk through it and straight onto a bus to Pocklington. There's no waiting around, the bus seems to be waiting for my return.

We see urban life as hectic and island life so calm; but is that really true? Back in civilisation everything is at our finger tips. Our streets are tarmaced, our paths solid, shops full of produce, everything we wish for provided for us. On the islands, life is a constant battle, a battle with the elements. On the mainland the wind and sea is not our master. Here we can jump on a bus or take a taxi without a second thought; our lives are so much easier and far more predictable. Yet, if our lives are so easy, why do we make them so difficult? We set ourselves goals, which only seem to cause us stress and criticize our neighbours, instead of working with them. On the islands you have to work together; you are more aware that you are all inter-dependant. But, here on the mainland whilst we think we are self sufficient, in reality this is not possible.

Although the islands have the harder life, they have a strong sense of purpose; a vision which draws their community together for the greater good. On the mainland, we have the easier life, yet there is no vision that binds us together as one. Which of the two really has achieved Utopia?

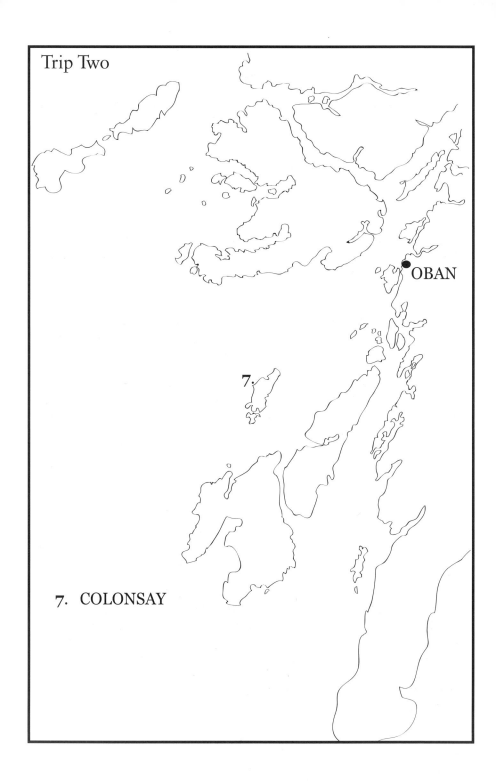

Trip Two

OBAN

7.

7. COLONSAY

4
CHRISTMAS CELEBRATIONS

THURSDAY 25TH DECEMBER 2003
TO FRIDAY 2ND JANUARY 2004

It is Christmas Day and my journey is continuing, this time I am not travelling alone. Ruth and I have hired a cottage for a week on the Hebridean island of Colonsay. So, I am moving up market, swapping my tent and stove for the luxury of self catering accommodation complete with lounge, bedroom, kitchen and bathroom.

It all feels very different, joining two parts of my life together; Ruth and my islands. But, tonight she too will look out at Kerrera and share some of the emotions I experienced back in September and that feels good.

Let me update you since I got back to Yorkshire in September. The major change, subject to the legal boys, is that I'm moving. Ruth and I are selling our two flats and buying a lovely three bedroom semi together. We think the house is just perfect, right out in the country with enough room for us to have our own space and accommodate all our bits and pieces. Mostly I am looking forward to having my own garage and being able to sit out in the garden and listen to the sounds of nature.

The car is packed fit to burst, with clothes, food, beer, gin, a microwave, a TV (Ruth's idea) and our children. I'm glad that I am not backpacking on this trip! Our children, in case you are wondering, are not the human kind. They are a collection of 22 teddy bears, each with its own colourful life. So, on this trip, Clyde is joined by his wife Bonnie and 20 of their friends!

Having said farewell to Yorkshire, we make really good time in reaching Oban. Not being a great one for driving in strange surroundings, I surprise Ruth and myself by sharing the driving for a 100 or so miles and actually quite enjoy it. As we leave Tyndrum the snow clad mountains start to surround us and conditions along the road to Oban make for slower driving. However, eventually the weather conditions improve and we reach Oban, just as dusk is starting to set in.

Back at the Oban Youth Hostel, I find that we have been given a family room all to ourselves. It is perfect for us, with its own ensuite facilities as well as access to a kitchen.

After a good night's sleep followed by a calm three-hour crossing, our ferry docks at Scalasaig, Colonsay; island number seven. This island, joined at low tide to Oronsay, has just over 100 inhabitants and is roughly ten miles long and two miles wide.

Garta Goban, our cottage, is at Port Mor on the west side of the island. It looks straight out onto the Atlantic, next stop Canada. We have rented it from the Isle of Colonsay Estate at a cost of £330 for the whole week. It is delightful, with spectacular views and a welcoming fire burning away on our arrival.

By the time we have unloaded all our belongings the day is slipping away, so we decide to take a quick drive round the island before daylight disappears altogether. Our circular route takes us past the Primary School and eventually drops us back down into Scalasaig, offering breathtaking views of the Paps of Jura in the distance. From here, past the island Surgery, Shop, Pier and Hotel, we arrive back at the cottage, after passing the island Golf Course on our left.

Refreshed after a great night's sleep, we awaken late. Today we plan to visit Kiloran Bay and Balnahard Bay to the north of the island. All kitted out with food and warm clothing, our walk begins by crossing Kiloran Bay. What a magnificent bay, it boasts a massive expanse of beach and strong Atlantic waves. It is evidently good for surfing too, but today we walk across it completely on our own. After a few miles walking, we sit and rest upon the rocks at Balnahard Bay. What good fortune it is to be able to sit and picnic amongst December sunshine, whilst enjoying views of Jura ahead and Mull to the left. I am so pleased to get back to my islands and heartened to see Ruth becoming quite adventurous too, clambering up and down the rocks on her way up here, making the most of all this rugged beauty.

Unfortunately, the good weather doesn't hold and, half way back to Kiloran Bay, we get caught in heavy rain. By the time we reach the car we are both soaking, having been subjected to biting cold hailstones and gusting winds. I've never experienced such ferocious winds before. We are both relieved to get back to the warmth of the cottage and to dry out our wet clothes on the old fashioned pulley above the fire.

The following day brings no improvement in the weather. We decide to make the most of our convivial surroundings, relax in front of the fire and make plans for our new home and the rest of our time on Colonsay. Today this cottage has distinct advantages from being in my tent!

As a new day breaks, we are delighted to see much better weather, clear skies and sunshine, which means that we can enjoy the drive into "town." The island shop in Scalasaig is a real treat, well stocked even with vegan goodies. When you come to an island like this you never know if the food supply caters for a vegan diet, which is why we brought our own; a real shame as we have deprived the island of some income. Enterprises are the life blood of an island and I am keen to support them wherever possible. However, one thing that I do purchase this trip is a CD by Donald MacNeill. Its words and music are inspirational, a very talented man.

My one regret is that, because we aren't here during a daytime low tide, we won't be able to walk the full distance across The Strand to Oronsay. Today we endeavour to walk as far as we can across ice-covered sand. What an amazing experience it is, watching the fragile ice crack and splinter, sending out thousands of tiny slivers amongst the sheet of thin ice; just like a giant spider's web. As the sun sets behind Oronsay its final rays set the ice alive, sending a golden glow which shimmers across the ice and sand. I have seen many beautiful sunsets in my life but this one has got to be amongst the finest.

After yet another good night's sleep, we awaken to dark clouds. Our stay on the island is drawing to a close and we are determined to walk today, whatever the weather. Our plan is to walk southwards across the Golf Course towards Ardskenish. I remember reading somewhere that Colonsay has a "challenging course". Challenging? With the full force of the Atlantic blasting across these fairways, the only winner here has got to be the wind!
By the time we return to the cottage we are completely wet through. But it has been great fun, and we have even managed to shelter behind a rock and treat ourselves to coffee and vegan Christmas cake along the way!

Having enjoyed a piping hot bath and dried out, tonight being Hogmanay, we head for the Colonsay Hotel advertised as the "most remote hotel in Great Britain". We stroll in expecting to fight our way to the bar. Give me strength. Am I in Scotland or a morgue? This place is dead apart from a few stockbroker type customers. What a load of miserable people and where are the locals? We have one drink and decide that it will be livelier bringing in the New Year together in our own cottage! However, being a couple of boring old farts, we are still in bed by 12.30am!

The big advantage of this is that we both awake early, hangover free. After breakfast, we take a leisurely drive around the island and are amazed that the etiquette of this morning's car drivers is almost none existent. Instead of the usual courteous stopping in passing places to let people past, today the drivers we meet are discourteous, impatient and determined not to let you through. We put this down to visitors arriving on the island for the New Year.

Indeed Colonsay, with all its beauty and remoteness, depends heavily on the tourist trade; this results in numerous challenges for the islanders as visitors try to manoeuvre their roads.

As our ferry leaves for Oban, we bid Colonsay farewell and start to look forward to life in our new home.

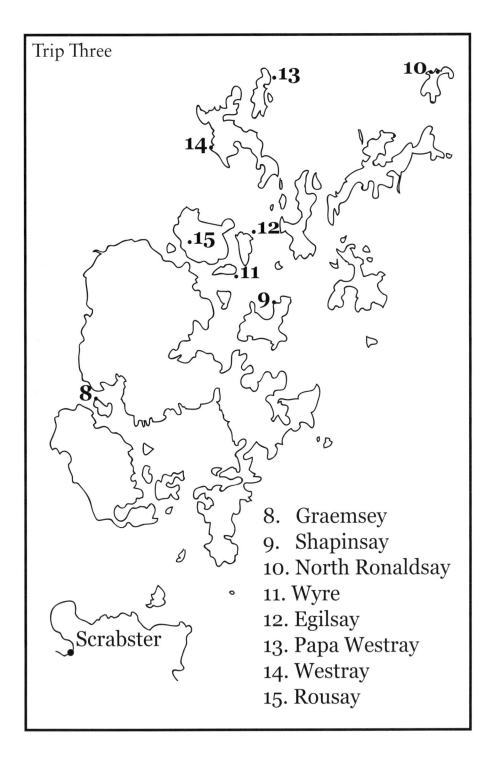

Trip Three

8. Graemsey
9. Shapinsay
10. North Ronaldsay
11. Wyre
12. Egilsay
13. Papa Westray
14. Westray
15. Rousay

Scrabster

5
THE ORKNEY

THURSDAY 1ST APRIL 2004
TO SATURDAY 17TH APRIL 2004

My islands beckon and once again it is time to head north. It's almost three months since Ruth and I returned from Colonsay. This time I am travelling on my own, apart from Clyde. Leaving our new home, for the first time, seems really strange; why would you want to leave paradise when you are so happy there? But I know that I have to move now, with the arrival of better weather, if I am ever to sleep on each of the 162 islands. So far I have visited nine of them and only slept on seven. I still have a long way to go.

Today I am back on the train and, after concerns for my personal health and safety, I have reduced my kit so that now I am carrying a considerably reduced backpack. I am excited and ready to go. My return ticket from York to Thurso has cost me £51; excellent value considering that my journey will be over 900 miles.

Yorkshire's countryside soon fades into the distance as I doze most of the way to Inverness. There, I end up in conversation with some new travelling companions from Wick. I reach Thurso at 9.30pm and check into a hostel which costs me the modest sum of £9 for a single room for the night. I am not that impressed. It receives my two out of ten rating, being just one step up from the Observatory at Spurn Point. Anyway, at least it is quiet, the tourist season does not seem to have started here yet.

Knowing that my taxi is booked for 5.30am I don't sleep very well. The Scrabster to Stromness ferry leaves at 6am and I am anxious in case my taxi doesn't turn up. I needn't have worried. It arrives on time and takes me the two mile journey to the ferry terminal. Here I am, at the top of Scotland. Wow, all the U.K. mainland is south of me! It is still dark and I can't see very much; but it does feel strange knowing that my country has come to an end!!

I am most impressed by the ferry, which is brand new, barely a year old. Such high standards and cleanliness. It has to be the most impressive ferry I have ever seen. As I say farewell to the mainland I look back and say a little prayer; a thank you for allowing me this trip to my islands. It is a very special moment and although the weather is poor, wet and windy, I feel so lucky to be here.

After such an early start I am in need of some sustenance. My plate of baked beans on toast, washed down by a piping hot cup of camomile tea, is just what the Doctor ordered. The journey to Stromness is not a long one, only taking an hour and a half in total; but we pass through the Pentland Firth, a fierce stretch of water whose reputation comes from its ferocious meeting of North Sea and Atlantic tides. It is too dark to see much, unfortunately, and justice is not done to the famous rock stack, the Old Man of Hoy, by this morning's dull, wet daybreak. One day I'll visit Hoy, hopefully in better weather conditions.

At 7.30am we dock at Stromness on the Orkney Mainland. It's like arriving at an airport with its impressive ferry walkway. The journey has been fantastic and all for £13. Absolutely amazing value.

The Graemsay ferry is leaving in five minutes. I have no chance to explore Orkney Mainland; but I will spend a night here some other time. My next ferry, with its crew of two, is considerably smaller than the one I have just got off. Today there are only two passengers aboard, myself and another man. The transfer seems to happen really fast and, in no time at all we are on our way, sailing back out towards Hoy. As we enter Hoy Sound I immediately become aware of the ocean. Our small boat starts to bounce up and down on the waves and my baked beans threaten mutiny deep within my stomach. We pull into the Bay of Quoys and the ferry makes its first stop at Moaness, to the north of Hoy; Ward Hill towering in the background. Wow! This island seems so remote with just a few cottages scattered in front of me, nestling into the hills. There is hardly a soul about.

Approaching Graemsay, island number eight, which lies at the western entrance to the Scapa Flow I am pleased to finally reach my destination. I watch my fellow passenger drive away in an exhaust blowing car, which was parked up waiting for him at the pier. This island which covers an area of about two square miles is very flat, with its highest point West Hill only 62 metres high. Its current small population of only 27 people is principally made up of crofters.

Battling against the wind, I follow the road towards the Bay of Sandside and find a place to put up my tent. Even though I am more sheltered here, it's still quite a struggle as the wind is so strong. Well, maybe the islanders consider this average but, for me, it is the windiest place I have ever had in which to set up a camp. A car goes by and the driver waves. He's the first person I've seen since arriving here, apart from my fellow passenger on the boat. My camp site looks out across the Bay of Sandside towards Orkney Mainland. It is a beautiful location with the splendid Hoy High Lighthouse to my right. Close to where I have camped is a small Community Hall, complete with water, toilet and a dry floor; an ideal location where I can roll up my tent or seek refuge if it looks like I'm going to get blown away during the night. All in all this is a real score!

Already I have requested my ferry for the morning; this is such an amazing service, these ferries often appear for just one passenger. Next to the Hall, on the road, is a solitary public phone box; complete with a brand new base. Unfortunately in spite of trying every combination of coin the phone doesn't work. Ah well the base looked good, all we need now is a BT engineer!

I decide to walk to the Hoy Low Lighthouse which is at the north west extremity of the island. Keeping me company along the way are flocks of curlews and lapwings. The song of the curlew reverberates so much around this island, I decide that it should be renamed "Curlew Island".

My walk takes me past several deserted ruined houses. I pause, fascinated by one of them. All that remains is its fireplace and chimney; devastated by these harsh conditions, nothing else is left standing. This island with its powerful wind feels bleak to me, certainly not a clearance feel but that of a steady decline. There are no trees here. Mind you, I'm not really surprised with this wind, and I have read that this is true of the Orkney as a whole.

Once I reach the far end of the island, I lie down in the grass, about 20 metres above the sea. It is comfortable and inviting, the grass feels like a sponge as I lie here listening to the sounds. The wind and the sharp rain don't bother me too much, I have fantastic equipment. I watch as the wind catches the birds, seemingly catapulting them downwards in its strong air currents. The birds seem to be completely at one with it all, adapting easily in these conditions.

I continue my walk, and am fascinated to come across a sight which appears to be from bygone days. There, resting on the bank, in the shelter of an old stone storehouse, is a dilapidated boat; it is almost hidden from view in the long grass. The boat is still attached by its rope to a rusty winch. Inside the storehouse are the remains of some equipment, including a pair of old yellow Wellington boots which are hanging from a nail, slowly rotting away. It is the first boat that I have seen on Graemsay, apart from my ferry.

As I make my way down the small slope of West Hill, heading towards Kirk Geo and the old island Kirk, I am amazed to see that all the sheep are following me. This seems really strange. Normally sheep are timid creatures and run if you come near them. Perhaps they think that I am going to feed them?

Today the old Kirk is used as a barn for storing hay; I guess it is fuller now than it ever was all those years ago. The graveyard with its epitaphs to the deceased, speaks volumes about the harshness of island life. One gravestone describes four children dying before their parents did; one dying at sea and another drowning. Other stories tell of a marine master, someone who died in New Zealand and someone who was interned in Stromness. What a life it must have been, the seas, emigration, an early death and jail. This graveyard is not a romantic fiction, it is a place of history and of hard times. Here I am, with my most advanced clothing and equipment, and I can still feel the harshness that our forefathers endured. What respect they deserve from us all.

With no Celtic Cross evident, this church yard is quite different from those in the Western Isles. I miss it, being drawn myself to the Celtic tradition. I don't get a strong sense of God in a traditional way on this island. Instead, I feel God in its harshness. Graemsay is only a small island and its beauty is in the harshness and sadness of decline. I pray that the spirit of Graemsay will return and that the island will become rejuvenated.

After a great night's sleep, I awaken feeling warm and peaceful. It is only 6.30am. It has been raining most of the night and the winds have been constant. As I peep out of my tent I can see some ducks, a type that I have never seen before, and a pair of oystercatchers circling my tent. I smile noticing my favourite, the seal; I spotted him last night. This morning he has come to the edge of the sand, we are only ten metres apart. Seals are such curious creatures.

I breakfast on baked beans and coffee and then make good use of the Community Hall to pack my tent. In this wind it is almost impossible to do so outside. Afterwards I walk slowly towards the pier for the 10.15am ferry. I love Graemsay with its small population, wind, seals, oystercatchers, birds that I don't know, curlews, lapwings and no tourists. As I sit in the pier waiting room, enjoying the heat from the storage heaters, I notice the splendid new telephone and disabled toilets; although I am not quite sure how disabled people get off the ferry and up the steep steps.

My ferry arrives five minutes early. On its journey back to Stromness I chat to a fellow passenger, who mentions that the population on Hoy is reasonably stagnant. People move onto the island, he says, but usually leave before or after two winters. So the population there just gets older.

After a coffee in Stromness, I catch the bus to Kirkwall. The 30 minute journey is wonderful, taking me past the Stones of Stenness. I feel a bit like a fisherman hitting port. Now it is time for some rest and recuperation; a few drinks and some essential shopping before I head back out to sea. The ferry to Shapinsay leaves at 2.15pm.

My short crossing north-east from Kirkwall to Shapinsay, island number nine, only takes about 25 minutes. Shapinsay is seven times bigger than Graemsay and has a population of around 300 people.

As I begin my search for somewhere to camp, I register that Shapinsay looks a reasonably flat island; although my backpack, complete with its new provisions tells me otherwise. After a walk of about three miles, I eventually find a suitable location on the Bay of Sandgarth; to the south-west of the island. As I begin to put up my tent, I ask myself why I persist in camping so near to the coast? The wind here is really strong and, before I know it, I have lost a tent peg. Tent manufacturers please note all tent pegs need to be painted in bright colours to prevent them getting lost in the grass! Eventually, after I have turned the air blue, I end up moving my tent and erecting it behind a very small bank. This is a far better arrangement. Orkney certainly seems to get plenty of wind, although to date the rain hasn't been too bad.

Now that I have set up my camp, I need some water. My search is unsuccessful and I am forced to draw it from a questionable dyke. I know it is stupid but what else can I do? I make myself a coffee and some food and then wash it down with a nip of whisky. Not too much you understand, but just enough for me to wonder whether I'm pissed or not? I suppose if I am even asking the question then the answer has got to be "yes"! Throwing all caution to the winds, I pour myself a second nip and lie back on the grassy bank, looking out onto a kelp covered beach which is adorned with birds searching for their evening meal. Soon the sun starts to drop in the sky. It is a magnificent sunset. I think to myself that really life is not too bad; and neither is this whisky.

I wake in the middle of the night, somewhat startled to find that the sea is now only six feet from my tent door! Fortunately the light from the moon is strong enough for me to assess the situation. I decide that I'm OK and go back to sleep.

Still alive to tell the tale, I set off at 8am to explore my surroundings. Shapinsay is a really interesting island. It reminds me of Holland, a picture of order and symmetry. Dykes down the side of each perfectly straight road and a grid system that divides the island into ten acre square fields. Evidently this system was introduced back in the 19th century by the Balfour family, in order to increase the islander's agricultural production. Today the land looks rich and fertile and I would say that life on Shapinsay is as good as any other island.

The island has a School, a Pub, which I've still to find, and a General Store that even opens for four hours on a Sunday. There don't seem to be any new cars about, but there is a Fire Station and, amazingly, a gritter!

Today's walk is about 15 miles long. I am heading north, first stopping off to look at Burrroughston Broch; an Iron Age site which looks out onto the Stronsay Firth. As I near the site, following the grassy path which leads to the mound, I am amazed to see, right in the middle of a mound, the broch. I've never seen one before. Peering down into it my thoughts drift back to how it must have been all those years ago. What an incredible place it is, tucked away so discreetly up here; what stories it could share with us all.

I continue my walk across the island, following these amazingly straight roads with their slight inclines. In front of me I can see Gairsay, just to the right of Orkney Mainland. It is one of the many islands I still have to visit.

By the time I reach Mill Dam, the RSPB nature reserve I have walked a good six miles. My legs are starting to ache and I am asking myself why on earth I have come all this way. But I am glad that I have made the effort, Mill Dam is most definitely worth the walk. The hide there is the best, it's as simple as that. It has a wonderful stock of binoculars and telescopes and also little binoculars for the children. I am most impressed with it. Mill Dam is home to thousands of breeding birds. I sit and watch a lapwing build her nest, I didn't realise they were so green.

On my way home, I call in at the General Store. All this walking has made me really thirsty and I've not had a drink since breakfast. I treat myself to four bottles of beer. This is perhaps not the best of ideas. I hurry up the lane and sit down. Before I know it I have drunk them all! So, as well as having four empty glass bottles to carry all the way back to my campsite, I am now also feeling slightly pissed.

Fortunately my legs carry me and the bottles home. En route I meet a really nice couple who own the B&B near to where I am camping. They tell me about the

Pub that I still haven't been able to find. It seems that their B&B is not a major earner but they are happy and contented with life.

I reach my tent and next fetch some more water from the dyke. All day long I haven't been able to find any clean water; the storage and carrying of water is something that I still need to look into. I cook my pinto beans and make a mental note not to buy them again. Then, after a cup of coffee, I fall asleep.

Shapinsay is a lovely tidy island. If Graemsay is "Curlew Island" then it is "Tidy Island."

After a comfortable night's sleep, I am up at 6.30am. My tent is wet, but it's too windy to put it away properly, so I just roll it up and place it on top of my backpack. My walk back to Balfour, where I catch the ferry, starts in light drizzle and ends with glorious sunshine. A pair of oystercatchers fly in front of me, leading the way. They are magnificent birds, a perfect couple. Sadly, it is time to say goodbye to Shapinsay.

I am in good time for the 10.30am ferry. In fact the 9.00am boat is only just pulling in, so I step onboard. It is full of construction workers. I get chatting to a Geordie who works on the ferry. Because of my accent he thinks I'm one too, so I soon put him straight! To me, the men who work on the ferries are the real men of these islands. My short journey across the water to Kirkwall is a time for reflection; I am comfortable with my thoughts whilst others chat away round about me.

Upn arriving back at Kirkwall ferry terminal, I head for the Shapinsay ferry waiting room and take out my tent to let it dry. Next I rearrange my pack and start to make plans for the next part of my journey. I decide that on Saturday I will fly to Papa Westray. It will involve taking the world's shortest scheduled flight; two minutes between Papa Westray and Westray. But first I am going to fly to North Ronaldsay.

I take the airport bus from Kirkwall. Orkney Airport is a wonderful experience. It is a breath of fresh air, not a policeman in sight and personal service of the highest order. A really helpful lady takes me through the whole process of buying my air tickets for Papa Westray and North Ronaldsay. What a lovely nature she has. Now all I have to do is wait, which in itself is most enjoyable. The relaxed contemplative atomsphere here makes me feel as though I am sitting in an art gallery. I look out from my seat towards the planes; well, there are two at one point.

Eventually it is time to board my plane. It's a bit like getting into a car, only this one has five rows of two seats. Having already flown considerably around the world, I have got to say that this is, without doubt, my most perfect plane journey ever and also my most comfortable trip. Flying towards North Ronaldsay, at just 4000 feet, the views today are spectacular. Below me I can see all my islands; all the islands of northern Orkney. Shapinsay looks so small from out of my window. I feel like a small child who has just opened his presents on Christmas Day, I am bursting with this feeling of wonderment and excitement. It has got to be my best plane journey ever.

At North Ronaldsay airport, my island number ten, we are met by Kevin; a bearded gentleman. "North Ron" is Orkney's most northerly island and measures three miles by one mile. It has a population of just under 60 people. Kevin, as well as being the island Doctor, also runs the North Ronaldsay Bird Observatory and in addition still finds time to fit in the lambing!

The Observatory, "Obs" Guest House, is situated at the south-west of the island at Twinyess. It is a new building with spectacular views out over the North Ronaldsay Firth. It is run by the kindest of people. My first evening meal of chilli, rice and salad is far more than I am expecting; washed down by a glass of beer from the well stocked bar I am truly delighted.

There are two other guests with me tonight at the "Obs", a father and his 11 year old son. After our meal the father asks the islanders one of the five standard questions that I have heard so many times already. It reminds me of my travels in India. How often I used to be bombarded with the same old questions. "What is your name? You married? Why you not married? Why you not have children? What is your religion? Tonight the father asks "How much is a house on North Ron?" A standard question you might think, but these islanders will have already been asked it 100 times before. It is as if our whole lives revolve around money, possessions and a dream that one day we will flee from the rat race and live happily ever after on a remote Scottish island. We need to broaden our thinking and try and develop different lines of conversation if we are to engage; instead of boring the pants off the people who live on these islands.

After a fantastic breakfast of toast, beans, tomatoes and delectable mushrooms, washed down with orange juice and real coffee, I set off for a walk around the North Ron coast. It is good to get outdoors again, after my first night sleeping inside for a while.

This island is unique with its' 19th century sheep dyke; a two metre high construction, which ensures that the island sheep stay on the seashore. The North Ron sheep are renowned as seaweed eating sheep and, as a result, their meat is famous for its particularly salty taste. It is also most unusual to be able to walk around an island keeping strictly to its coastline. My walk today will be 13 miles long.

I realise that my walk is going to be quite challenging as it involves climbing over rocks on the seashore and slipping about on all the seaweed. As I reach South Bay I see my first seaweed eating sheep. Compared to the ones back in Yorkshire they seem very small and thin; varying in colour from black to cream with shades of grey to brown in between! They are extremely timid, bolting away the minute I start to get anywhere near them.

As I round the corner at Strom Ness and walk towards the next Bay, Brides Ithy, I am thrilled to see a colony of common seals lazing on the rocks. I get so close that I am almost tempted to stroke them, but I think twice about it. I learn later that they have a vicious bite, so I am glad of my sixth sense! Along the rocky beach, oystercatchers scurry in search of their next meal and pairs of fulmars fly low over the sea, before gliding upwards into the sky on another current of air. I'm told that when fulmars are nesting they defend their nests by spitting out a foul smelling oil which is virtually impossible to wash off.

My walk takes me northwards past Linklet Bay to Dennis Head, the home of Old Beacon, the island's old lighthouse which was finally extinguished in 1809. It is still in relatively good condition. But here the island has a real outpost feeling with powerful waves from the sea crashing against the rocks. I squat behind a wall at the top of the Orkney Islands and have a drink and a bite to eat. As I am squatting on my haunches, watching the fulmars swooping down on me, it starts to rain.

I continue walking to the most northerly point of the island, Point Sinoss, where North Ron boasts Britain's tallest land based lighthouse tower which is 42.3 metres high. There's also a fantastic whale watching hide here. I don't see any whales today but I really enjoy sitting in it just watching the amazing waves. I love this feeling of being on an outpost; knowing that I have come as far as I possibly can, separated from another country only by water. Here to my east the next stop is Norway and directly north, the Shetland Islands. To me, the Shetlands seem like another country, as yet unseen; hopefully I'll visit them soon and share their magic, as they too become part of my island journey.

I make my way back to the Obs. Time for a few beers and some Pringles. Today is the funeral of a lady who had spent her whole life on the island. She was 89 years old when she finally passed. A few of the islanders come back to the Obs Bar for a drink. I find it quite difficult understanding the accent of the Orkney folk, sometimes only managing to pick out one word in three. As I listen to them, it occurs to me that the real Orcadians, the people of the Orkney islands, were working class stock. They lived off the land in the hardest of conditions. Yet, today it is the middle class who are moving up here to retire. How will they fare in the harshest of climates?

After another excellent evening meal, I join the locals watching a game of football on T.V. Tonight it is Arsenal – v – Chelsea. It is like being at the cinema, gazing at their giant screen, five foot by six foot, which has been lowered from the ceiling. Chelsea win the match.

All in all it has been another memorable day.

Refreshed from the luxury of a good night's sleep and an enjoyable breakfast, I spend some time reading through the local papers. These give me some bits of information which I can use to plan the remainder of my trip. It's surprising how quickly my plans change.

Afterwards I take a short stroll to Hollandstoun where the island School and Kirk are both situated. First I stop and take a look around the Kirk. The newish white stone building has a most welcoming feel to it. It is quite sparse inside; set amongst this beautiful churchyard, it is quite in keeping with its surroundings. From here I walk past the Post Office cum Pub, then the School, after which I start to make my way back towards the Obs, where I meet a local lad who is just home from University. Soon we are joined by two electricians who are working on the school. We have a few beers and some good hearted banter. Ruth phones and the phone is brought to me, what service! It's good to chat to her although I'm a little pissed! Ah well I'm on holiday and on my islands, so it's fine, I know she understands.

Another perfect evening meal is served, they do so well here with my vegan diet. Then there's another football match after which it's time to sleep. Although today has been much less active than yesterday, it has still been perfect.

Today I am moving onto my next island. I have loved my stay in North Ron, but now it is time to say goodbye and to settle my bill. My total bill at the Obs is only £89.50; what amazing value. This includes laundry, beer, Pringles, B&B

and an evening meal for three days. I would like to see a place where I can get better value.

The front six acre field is being ploughed by the lad I met yesterday. He is getting paid £14 per acre. I don't know whether this is good pay or not? It's now 9.40am and my flight is due at 10.30am, we are leaving for the airport in about 20 minutes. It has been good to come in from the nature for a chance to shower etc. but now it is even better to be going back out into it again. Nature is the nearest that I can get to understanding God. For amongst nature; especially in the wind, I feel whole. The more I retreat from the material world, the more I am one with myself and my surroundings.

I arrive at the airport 20 minutes before departure. No one checks me, my luggage or my tickets, or even enquires whether I have one! Unfortunately, the flight is not as good as my journey up here; today it is misty and slightly bumpy. I am seated behind the pilot. Back in the terminal building at Kirkwall I suddenly realise that my Swiss army knife was in my pocket throughout the journey.

After replenishing my supplies in town, I take the bus to Tingwall where I catch the ferry to Wyre. Kirkwall has a good feel to it, but I am looking forward to getting back into nature and the outdoors.

The day continues to be misty and wet. My ferry sails into Wyre Sound and I step off onto Wyre, island number 11, around 3.30pm. This small island with its population of 14 people is about two square miles in size. At the pier I notice in large print the word "CANNA". Evidentally, 15 years ago Cal Mac helped out on this ferry route and the guys left their mark as a reminder; a little like the writing on the pier wall at Canna. Nice one.

I walk in a south-westerly direction, in search of a suitable camp site for the night. At Testaquoy Farm I meet the farmer and his wife and we end up chatting for over an hour. They kindly say that I can camp on their land; the mist is bad but I love it.

It's now 6.30pm and getting dark. I realise that this is only because of the mist. There are a few hours of daylight left, so I can still make the most of this short time to explore. It doesn't normally get dark until 9.00pm.

I am up early with the dawn, there's lots to do before I catch the 8.20am ferry to Egilsay. I pack my kit, roll up my tent and take it up to the Heritage Centre where I spread it out and let it dry. What an interesting place this is, with an exhibition about life on Wyre, photographs and memories from years gone by and sections on Cubbie Roo. There's a lot of hard work gone into it and is certainly a credit to the islanders.

I also manage to fit in a visit to Cubbie Roo's castle. I love that name, it sounds like an Australian mammal. Cubbie Roo was a Viking Chieftan who lived on Wyre in the 12th century and this castle was his stronghold. Very impressive it is too. Close to the castle stands St. Mary's Chapel. I take the opportunity to wander around the churchyard. Wyre is a lovely island; the smaller an island, the more I seem to like it.

After finally packing away my tent I sit in the ferry terminal waiting for my transport to arrive. This waiting room cost £15,000 for fourteen people.

It is an enjoyable trip to Egilsay. Travelling with me today is also a B.T. van and some decorators. Being Good Friday, I guess everyone must be on time and a half! I'm quite surprised when the boatman seems impressed that I camped out last night. I realise that my journey is more hardy than I had first thought and begin to feel proud of what I am doing.

At 9.00am my ferry sails into Rousay Sound and docks at Skaill pier. I am now on Island number 12, Egilsay. Slightly bigger than Wyre, Egilsay is three miles long by one and a quarter miles wide. It has a population of 26 people.

After disembarking I wonder where to put my tent. I have an early start again in the morning, so decide to camp near to the pier. Another advantage of this arrangement is that, in the morning, I will be able to dry out my tent in the pier waiting room. Once my camp is erected I set off to explore Egilsay.

I've not gone very far when I meet a man on a quad bike. He tells me that he has 12 children. In fact, his family make up half of the island's population! They are aged between 1 and 18 and he has home educated them all, until at 14 they go to the Grammar School on the mainland. They get by he says. Like North Ronaldsay, eggs are popular and his family can get through a few. I bet!

I also learn that there is an RSPB Reserve on Egilsay, in fact a lot of this island is a nature reserve. It offers ideal conditions for the corncrake, which is expected any day from the warmer climes of Africa. Whilst I am unlikely to see a corncrake, it seems that you are more likely to hear it at night.

I have a wonderful walk across the island which takes me past a flock of sheep, through meadows and across wet lands. In some places the ground water is four to five inches deep. I am fortunate, with my new decent pair of boots, that this doesn't really affect me. I walk on, passing a kissing gate which is tied up. All around me it is a bird watcher's paradise. There are terns, oystercatchers, swans, ducks, geese and so many more that I haven't a clue what they are.

Reaching the north of the island, I gaze out towards the small fishing boats in the Westray Firth, beyond them Westray, one of my islands. Across to the east is Eday. They are all so near to me here. I feel elated at this thought.

I make my way back to my tent and cook up some food. God, it is getting boring. By way of a treat, I tuck into a little bit of chocolate and have a nip of whisky in my coffee. I fall into a hazy sleep and wake up feeling even worse.

I could not visit this island without stopping off to see St. Magnus Church. It stands on a ridge in the centre of the island looking out towards Rousay Sound, conspicuous to anyone who arrives here. Egilsay is the place where Saint Magnus, Patron Saint of the Orkney Islands, was killed in 1117. It is thought that the beautiful ruined church was built as a shrine to him. It is the only surviving round towered church in Orkney and is still reasonably well preserved. I wander around the graveyard reading about the people who are buried here. It's starting to get cold, so I decide to retire with my diary and bottle of Scapa whisky, to the ferry waiting room.

Do you know, today I saw two lamas on Egilsay. You never know what is going to appear around the next corner.

I awake at 5.30am, my ferry is ordered for 7.20am. It will be my second ferry booking of the trip and, for the first time in five nights, my tent is dry.

On this adventure to visit all my islands, physical and mental energy is vital. It is interesting observing my different states of mind during the journey. The clever part is to remind myself that everything is transitory, which is fine in theory but in practice not quite so easy.

After breakfast, I repack my kit and walk the few metres to watch my ferry sail in towards the pier. A ferry just for me! It is an incredible thought. I am so grateful to the ferry company and the men who offer this wonderful service. My ferry first calls in at Rousay, before it heads towards Tingwall. Rousay seems so big compared with Egilsay and Wyre. I am not drawn to it. As the boat pulls out of Wyre Sound, I can see in the distance, to my right, the uninhabited island of Eynhallow and to my left, Gairsay. The thought of visiting an island like Eynhallow captivates me. Excited at the prospect of this future adventure, I watch day breaking over the Orkney and think to myself that the only real way to travel on a ferry is in the open air.

I don't have long in Kirkwall, 13 minutes in fact, just long enough to do a quick food shop and jump on the Airport bus. This time my check-in at Kirkwall Airport is not as straightforward as when I last visited. I am advised that I cannot fly with a gas cannister in my backpack. Oh shit! My flight leaves in 10 minutes. No worries, I can leave my gas and stove with the check-in staff and collect it on my return. Ultimately, this leaves me with no way of cooking my food on Papa Westray. So, after re-packing my kit, I am left with two minutes to sprint out the airport door, along the tarmac and onto the plane. As I jump on board I hear the door being secured behind me. Phew! Still catching my breath in my seat, the 10 seater plane soars up into the sky and I chuckle to myself reflecting how this incident would have been handled at Heathrow?

Papa Westray, island number 13, is affectionately known as Papa, meaning Priest. Lying 20 miles north of Kirkwall, about four miles long and a mile wide, it has 70 inhabitants.

With no camping gas, I'm now in need of some accommodation. There is a Youth Hostel at Beltane, not far from where the School is, and I get myself booked in there. It's quiet with only two ladies and two German men booked in at the moment.

It has turned into a glorious sunny day, so I decide to walk around the south of the island. I start my walk by paying a visit to St. Ann's Church, which is just down the road from where I am staying. It's quiet and, before I know it, I have nodded off, obviously in need of some spiritual rest and recuperation. Eventually, I awake feeling rejuvenated and ready to continue my walk.

As I head south my spirits start to soar. My route is taking me across some wonderful soft grassland which makes for easy walking. It's a perfect day, brilliant sunshine and not too much wind. Shortly, the Loch of Saint Tredwall begins to opens up to my right and I am able to see traces of Saint Tredwall's Chapel, which stands on its own, a mound situated on a small peninsular of the Loch.

Rounding the Loch and heading back towards the Youth Hostel, I first pass some Shetland ponies and then a herd of black Aberdeen Angus cattle. The latter, with yellow tags through their ears, look as if they are sporting trendy earrings. They are completely non-plussed by me. Back on my walk, I soon stop again, firstly to marvel at an old tractor which is ingeniously advertising, in bright red paint, the location of the farm post box, and then afterwards, a traditional old farm cottage, protected from the harsh elements by a solid stone roof. All these combine to form the very essence of Papa Westray; the part that never reaches the tourist literature.

Farming is the main activity for these islanders. I am interested to come across a small Bothy museum, at Holland Farm. It is a traditional stone building, including a dove cot, horse tramp mill, old tractor and a kiln. I spend quite some time looking around it. Then, having just read about the Knap of Howar on the west of the island, I decide to visit it for myself. It is the site of the oldest preserved house in northern Europe which dates back over 5,000 years ago.

The site is such an atmospheric place, tranquil and peaceful. I find the house easily; it is beneath the ground, surrounded on all sides by grass. The only openings, facing out towards the sea, are through low doors. As I stand there, looking out onto the calm waters of Papa Sound, a small plane flies overhead. I point my camera skywards and take its picture. I am suddenly struck by the uniqueness of what I have captured. Through my lens, I have witnessed the world's shortest scheduled flight passing high above. Such a very modern sight, framed alongside the oldest domestic property in northern Europe. The plane's, record breaking, two minute hop between Papa Westray and Westray is shorter in distance than the main runway at Heathrow. What a surreal picture.

I make my way back to the Youth Hostel, where I wash my hair and clean up. Afterwards, feeling much fresher, I decide to pay a visit to the island's Community Shop. These shops are so important to the islands; central points where the locals can stock up on provisions and catch up with the latest news. This one opens for 15 hours a week. I suppose with a population of 70 people it is long enough. The range and quality of food on sale here is most impressive; it is a vegan's paradise with vegan chocolate; tofu; oat cakes; soya milk and there is even vegan pitta bread on offer! I leave with a lighter wallet, quite a few nice little nibbles and also a bottle of Highland Park, which is from the northernmost Scotch whisky distillery in the world.

It turns out that tonight, being Saturday, is the only "Bar" night of the week. The Shop, Hostel, "Bar" and Guest House are all part of the same building and because it is a drunken night, fortunately I do not have too far to walk home afterwards!

After a drunken man's sleep, I awake to Easter Sunday on the Orkney. Here it is not as religious as on the Western Isles. My friendly German room mates inform me that I was snoring last night; not much, just a little. Fortunately they are leaving the hostel today, so soon I will have the dormitory all to myself, paradise.

I decide that today I'm going to explore North Hill Nature Reserve, which is about two miles from the Youth Hostel. North Hill is the highest point of the island. This Reserve is managed by the islanders who work in conjunction with Scottish Natural Heritage and the RSPB. Evidently it is a great place to see Arctic Terns, although I am told that they don't arrive here for a few weeks yet.

I am not disappointed. The Reserve is well worth a visit, particularly Fowl Craig which is a most spectacular cliff nesting site. It is also the place that the last Great Auk, a flightless relative of the puffin, was shot in 1813. I find it a captivating place and sit there for ages staring at a magnificent rock archway which has been worn away by the sea. Channelled through the eons of time it is now covered with colonies of sea birds. Spellbound, I watch as wave after wave crashes powerfully against it, creating a massive spray which exhilarates me whilst temporarily obliterating everything in sight. This cliff walk is spectacular; it has got to be one of the best cliff walks I've ever taken; accompanied by Shags, Fulmars and many other species of birds that still remain nameless to me.

I feel that my love for these islands is becoming my vocation. When I am on an island my soul connects with it and I start to come alive. For me the essence of each island is without doubt its coast. As I sit here alone, on top of Fowl Craig's splendid cliffs, I gaze out at the expanse of water beyond, and know that I am completely at one with myself and that which is greater. This is a wonderful day.

Sadly, I leave the cliff tops behind and start to make my way back towards Beltane, detouring to stop and visit St. Boniface's Kirk. Here is one of the oldest sites of Christianity in Orkney, dating back to the 12th Century. It is a beautifully restored building which is still regularly used today.

As I head back towards the Youth Hostel I meet a German gentleman who lives on the island. He tells me that there are 1,200 visitors a year to Papa Westray. I am amazed that there are so few. This is such a gem of an island. Further along a car stops to offer me a lift back to Beltane. It is the people from the Gospel Hall; I had called in there at the start of my walk this morning. In spite of their kindness, I decide that it is really too nice a day to be riding in a car.

The Youth Hostel is empty when I return. I find it hard to believe that I am experiencing such wonderful facilities here all by myself. It is so accessible too; only £12 for the return flight from Kirkwall. That fare price is absolutely incredible! Evidently, during the summer school holidays Beltane does get busy. But now? Where is everyone? Settled back in, I get my journal up to date, cook some food, do some packing and contemplate how incredibly lucky I am.

After a good night's sleep, I check out of the hostel early and walk to Moclett. It is at the south of the island and is where I am due to catch my ferry to Westray. As I reach the pier, I see it. Not my ferry, but a boat; a beautiful white yacht to be exact. Not major in size but big enough, with a small dinghy moored behind. It's 8.30am, a dry morning and not a soul is in sight.

I sit in the pier waiting room and watch it. It could take me to my islands. I contemplate my adventure. Do I wish that yacht and dinghy were mine? Materialism? Not interacting with my fellow man? Definitely not!

What absolute rubbish! Of course I do! In a way I guess I'm somewhere between materialism and minimalism. For me, I suppose it's a case of having what I need. The yacht? Well I could visit more islands, but then most probably I wouldn't be able to land and sleep on them. So after this debate, I decide that I would prefer to be without the yacht; although acknowledging that it would have had its uses.

The next thing I know it's 9.25am and the ferry is here. I have fallen asleep! I hurry down to the pier, only to find out that, because it is a Bank Holiday, the ferry is working as a charter boat. But "no worries, just hop on board." Once on deck I get talking to the couple who have chartered it. Amazingly they come from Scarborough, which is just up the road from where Ruth and I live. It also turns out that the man is a Leeds United fan. At this point his wife wanders off to talk to the boatman!

At the end of the crossing we dock at Gill Pier, in the Bay of Pierowall, Westray. This is my island number 14. I agree to pay a third of the charter costs, which works out at only £8. Two Yorkshire men, agreeing a price for a boat crossing; a Scottish boatman waiting for his money. There has got to be a punch line in there somewhere, but, for once in my life, I am at a loss for words!

Westray, the largest of Orkney's North Isles, is five times bigger than Papa

Westray and has around 600 inhabitants.

After saying farewell to my two fellow passengers, I phone the Bis Geos Hostel to sort out some accommodation. "That's fine. The lady won't be there but you can let yourself in and just make yourself at home." Such trust in this part of the world, it never ceases to amaze me. Next I do a bit of shopping, a few vegetables and some other nibbles. It is so nice to get some vegetables after living on a protein and carbohydrate diet for a few days.

My walk to the Hostel proves to be quite exhausting; it's about three miles from Pierowall, mainly in an uphill direction! But my exertions are well rewarded. The hostel is set in a beautiful location with views across the bay towards Rousay and the Orkney Mainland in the distance. I am relieved to finally put down my backpack and provisions. Soon Alena, a lovely lady who I spoke to earlier on the phone, arrives. As it will take a little time to get the hostel ready, I decide to go for another walk.

I head towards Noup Cliffs which is a RSPB Nature Reserve, to the north-west of the island. The Noup cliff tops hold Orkney's largest "seabird city". Evidently 40,000 guillemots, about one fifth of the entire Orkney bird population, reside here and I can quite believe it, when listening to this magnificent chorus of bird sounds.

In particular I love to watch the guillemots. They are a little like penguins, only up a cliff instead of on an ice cap at the South Pole. It is good to rest here, watching these charming black and white birds flapping their wings like crazy, before crash landing into the sea. They help to bring me some inner peace after my early start and all the walking I have done today.

I arrive back at the Hostel just as Alena is about to leave it. "All your bags are in your room, pay me tomorrow" she says as she heads for the door. It is good to have some time to myself. I am feeling my mental and physical energy starting to slip as I approach the end of my trip. Strangely I am also finding Westray unsettling. Definitely I prefer the smaller islands which seem to touch my soul in a way that these larger ones cannot.

Just as I am starting to feel more settled and enjoying the challenge of producing a vegetable curry, the phone rings. It is Alena. "An Art Group is calling at the Hostel tonight, is that O.K. with you?" "Yes, no problem. It will be interesting." I finish my curry. It is the best one I've ever made.

After a phone call from Ruth, followed by my eating a kiwi fruit and a full packet of Bourbon biscuits, the Art Group arrives. They turn out to be a really pleasant crowd of people and I end up enjoying my time with them. After they have gone I settle back down to listen to Bob Dylan on the hostel CD player and enjoy a few glasses of whisky. I have the place to myself. It has got to be the highest standard hostel I've ever seen; adorned with nets, sails, ropes and nautical maps; it has a real Orcadian feel.

Waking around 7am I peer out of my dormitory window. It looks wet and windy outside, certainly not the best of weather. I am still in need of recharging my batteries, so I decide that I will enjoy a "me day". I hardly have time to savour this thought when I am joined by some more hostellers; a couple, their friend, five children and a little dog. They will be joining me in the dormitory. Isn't it funny how life often brings you the opposite of what you think you need? As a single person, generally my life is quiet and orderly so, a "me day" accompanied by five children is quite a different experience! Still, I guess it's healthy to see how other people live, just for a short period of time! I spend the day chatting with them all, generally putting the world to rights and drinking whisky. Fortunately they are a decent crowd of people and we seem to get on well.

At 10pm I go to sleep. These larger islands are not for me.

After a night's sleep, interrupted by my roommate's snoring, I take the ferry from Westray back to Papa Westray. It feels so good to be back. How I love the intimate feel of the smaller islands. As I am two hours early for my flight back to Kirkwall, I take shelter at St. Boniface's church, where I write up my journal. Completed, I sit quietly, enjoying the peace within this beautiful old Kirk.

Papa Westray Airport is a hive of activity today. I am surprised to see three African gentlemen, the only black faces I've seen in the Orkney, who are also leaving the island on my flight. After attending a Conference in Edinburgh, they have made the journey north to Papa. These men, who are used to seeing the birds of Papa in drab African plumage, have been thrilled to witness the same birds now resplendent in new Spring outfits. Their visit has been the focal point of recent island activity; indeed, many islanders have played a part in their welcome. Some have lent clothing to help them keep warm in the harsher climate and the island's children have even got in on the act, downloading African flags for the welcome of their important guests. All in all it has been a wonderful opportunity for everyone to learn about their visitor's very different countries, cultures and religions.

We have perfect conditions for our flight back to Kirkwall via Eday. Eday's airport lies to the west of the Bay of London and is consequently named London Airport. At Kirkwall I am reunited with my gas canister and stove, including the offer of the box it was stored in. Heathrow beat that!

It seems strange to be back on the mainland. Here, everyone is so presentable, not a pair of walking boots in sight. I stop off at a café opposite the Cathedral for a bite to eat, but find it soulless. Afterwards I catch the bus to Tingwall, where I spend some time looking around for a boat that can take me to Eynhallow. There is nothing. The uninhabited island of Eynhallow is turning out to be quite a challenge. I am also recognising that asking for help at the Tourist Information Centre is pointless, because they are more geared towards mainstream tourism. I begin to realise that getting to the uninhabited islands is going to be the biggest challenge on this journey. So, rather dejectedly, I decide to visit Rousay.

During my 30 minute journey from Tingwall to Rousay, as the ferry is taking me across the Eynhallow Sound, I can see the small elusive island in the distance, tucked in just to the left of Rousay. Eynhallow looks small and flat in comparison to my island number 15. Rousay measures five square miles and is home to 250 people. As the ferry pulls into the slipway at Trumland I become aware of the height of the island.

Fortunately I don't have far to walk to the island Hostel; an organic working farm which is close to the pier. Yet again I find that I have the place to myself. This Hostel is more basic than the one on Westray and I would certainly hate to be here when it's full; but as it stands, having the run of the place for £8 a night can't be too bad.

I am feeling sociable, so I make my way to the local Pub which is near to the pier. Celtic are on the TV. They are playing in the quarter final second leg of the UEFA Cup in Spain losing 2-0 to Villarreal. In spite of their defeat it ends up being a good evening in the Pub. I make the mistake of sitting at the bar, with my third drink and, as a result, find myself staggering back to the Hostel some hours later, decidedly worse for wear.

I crawl out of bed around 9.30am. God, I feel rough. Well, what a surprise after consuming half a bottle of Highland Park last night! I rack my brain trying to remember it all. I can recall most of the journey home, but not actually getting into my sleeping bag. I suppose that's not too bad.

Eventually around 10.30am, after dosing myself with aspirins and water, I set off on what I reckon must be a 14 mile walk around the island. The way I am feeling, I must be mad. The route I plan to take will be circular around the island, albeit following a single track in places.

I have been walking for a couple of miles when I come across a phone, and decide to give Ruth a call. As I pick up the receiver I notice, tucked into the stone wall, a card for the island taxi service. What great marketing! I am tempted to call it, but decide to keep going. After joining the Westness Walk, which is described as the most important archaeological mile in Scotland, I am amazed to come across a Swedish Consulate at Westness House! Who knows, maybe there are plans to open a new "Ikea" here!

My walk takes me directly opposite Eynhallow and, for the first time, I am able to get a better look at it. It is only about half a mile across the water from Rousay; so close that I can almost reach out and touch it. It certainly fascinates me, this small uninhabited island, but how will I ever get there?

I notice, in the distance, also following the Westness Walk, a group of walkers complete with umbrellas! How they manage to stop them from blowing inside out in this weather I'll never know. They are obviously heading towards the Midhowe Broch, which I have decided to give a miss. Old buildings don't do a great deal for me.

I am far more interested to learn about the Rousay clearances. These took part in the mid 19th century when 200 of the island's crofters that lived in Westness and Quandale, were driven from their land, reputably, by the worst landlord in the Orkney. These two areas were the only places in the Orkney to suffer from the clearances. Throughout Scotland, during the 1800's, landlords cleared their lands of small tenant farmers to make way for larger, more profitable sheep farms. The helpless victims were either forced onto different land, or to emigrate, forming part of the brave New World, where their ancestors still reside today.

Last night, in the Pub, I was also told about the blow holes which are to be found at the north of the island. Never having seen one before, I am determined to see what they look like. So here I go, over one fence, through some boggy heather, up to the top of some cliffs, across pastureland. I peer down and ..... Wow! Now I understand why the Tourist Information Centres don't list them. Up here it would be the easiest thing for someone to slip and fall. They are a Health and Safety expert's worst nightmare.

My first blow hole is about three metres across. From the top, it looks just like a chimney, and at the bottom, where the sea comes in, is where the fire would be. Although the sea doesn't blow all the way up the stack today, the power of the sea is still immense. I walk on a little further, stopping twice to lie on my stomach and peer through the narrowest of crevices into the thunderous waters below. Then I come across my next blow hole. Oh my God! It has got to be one of the most amazing things I have ever seen. It is about five metres across with two holes which are between eight and ten metres deep. If I slip I don't fancy my chances. I guess the best that I could hope for would be an air sea rescue. Perhaps I ought to invest in a mobile? Ah, maybe not, life has to have some risk.

As my walk is following a circular path, my horizons are constantly changing. I find it exciting to be treated to the ever changing views of Rousay's many island cousins. Long after Eynhallow and Orkney Mainland have disappeared from view, I am treated to glimpses of Westray, Faray, Eday, Egilsay and Wyre. As the west side of Eday starts to appear on the horizon, my walk takes me up a slow, gradual incline. It has been a long walk and my legs are starting to pull. But the views from the top of this hill make it well worth the effort. I look out across all my islands, some that I've conquered, some that I've not. Each one looks so inviting, calling me to come and take a better look. What an incredible walk this has been.

As I descend, Egilsay reappears. Rousay is a big island, the 19th largest of the 162, yet it has been a manageable walk. I return to the hostel, still amazed to find no other guests there. I shower, wash my hair and shave and then deliberate on what culinary delight I will enjoy tonight. "What about baked beans old boy? What a great idea!"

I read a little and contemplate a lot. Tonight is the last night of what has proved to be an amazing trip. It has all turned out far better than I had ever hoped. I have visited nine more islands and most importantly gained some contacts for future island visits.

Today, it is time for me to say "goodbye" to Orkney. I awake early after only a few hours sleep and join the Rousay school children on the 7.45am ferry to Tingwall. As our journey then continues, by bus from Tingwall to Kirkwall, I start to think about "the rat race". Many islanders talk about escaping "the rat race" but here their children need a car, a ferry and one or two buses to get to school and then, at the end of a long day, they have to make the same journey home. Don't believe that remote island life is always Utopia.

After stopping in Kirkwall for a vegetable curry at the Chinese Restaurant, I catch the final bus of the day to Stromness, where I join the ferry back to the UK mainland.

My crossing is full of mixed emotions. As I sail past Graemsay, I look towards the beach which was my first Orkney home and remember the soft grass where I laid back and fell in love with the Orkney. It seems so strange to be going home. Home is here, on my islands, yet my home is in Yorkshire. I am not a nine to five man, I am a travelling man. A mortgage, a career, a pension plan, can I give it all up to live an island life? Will that ever be possible?

My island journey will continue. It is time to head south; such a long way between Yorkshire and North Ronaldsay. The power which is evident within these islands; the power within nature, the seas, the people and the past, all draws me to where I want to be. As long as I feel this power, this energy, then I will continue my journey.

On my train journey south I meet a lovely lady called Sally, who gives me some advice about writing a book. It is quite a thought, but right now it is secondary to what I am hoping to achieve. What the end result will be is not important; means are never justified by the ends. To reach the end, the means have to be true.

So, it is with a heavy heart that I reach home. I need to work, to earn, to pay my bills and I need to plan for my next trip. I have a life in Yorkshire and, more especially, I have my partner Ruth. But to say goodbye to my journal seems so sad, for when I stop my writing I lessen my connection with my islands, with God and with my soul. But goodbye it has to be for the time being. It is time to pack away my journal and continue with my mainland life.

6
BIRTH OF ISLAND MAN?

APRIL 2004

To My Island Man.....

With flowing locks and handsome face, towards the hills he sets his pace.
With staff in hand through bracken treads, no stag or beastie does he dread.
He loves to watch the birds o'er land and oystercatchers in the sand.
His clan is from a far off land, where men work hard with calloused hand.
But here's his heart and that's right grand.
Oh how I love my Island Man.

Ruth

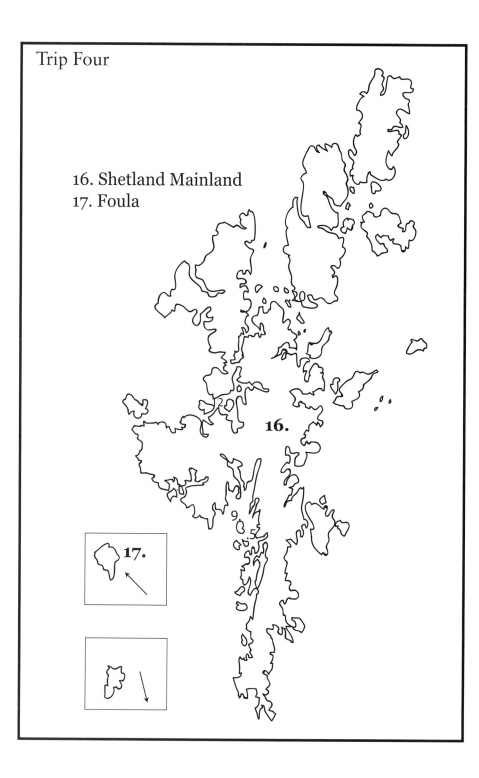

Trip Four

16. Shetland Mainland
17. Foula

16.

17.

7
END OF THE DREAM

Trip number four, 15 islands completed and only 147 to go!

Let me update you on my life since I returned from the Orkney. My business is going well and the order books are looking good. On a sadder note, my Grandma passed away. It was the first death in my family in 25 years. I didn't go to the funeral. I thought that, with my family situation, it was best to keep away; I know Grandma would have understood. The other major news is that Ruth and I have married; six and a half years since we first met. This doesn't mean a lot more to me than the formalisation of our relationship; I have been married to Ruth in heart, body and soul since the day I met her. Our wedding was just a small affair; it was what we both wanted. Organised in only 16 days, our special day was attended by 16 people, including ourselves. The two major differences the wedding has made is firstly, that the law officially recognises our union and secondly, that we both now wear a ring, a symbol of our love. I wear mine with pride.

My current thoughts about my island journey? Many people say how special Iona is. This is true, yet all the small islands have this special feel. It is just that, for most people, Iona is probably the only small island that they will ever visit. Tomorrow it is 60 years since D-Day. In 1944 those young men, who answered their country's call, had adventure in their souls and the strongest sense of duty to King, Country, family and to God. Today, the adventure I face is the call of my islands and, if I don't give it my all, it will be an insult to those brave men. I have been blessed with the gifts of time, money and health and I must use these gifts wisely. I often liken my island adventure to a jigsaw with 162 pieces. Who knows if there will be one or two pieces missing at the end? But, by then, the picture I will see will be much clearer than the one before me now. As the heroes of D-Day set forth they had absolutely no idea of what their final picture was to look like, and neither do I.

Ruth drops me off at York Station; it is a perfect goodbye to my wife….my wife.

We touch each others rings. Wearing this ring, I know we are closer than the miles can say.

The weather is fine and sunny with a reasonable forecast for the next few days. The only bad weather today is, would you believe, affecting the Northern Isles of Scotland? But of course!

The train to Aberdeen is old but comfortable. As I sit in Coach D, the silent coach, I am able to slow my thoughts down and start to switch off after the busy preceding few days. Past Edinburgh, the train lights give up the ghost, so my fellow passengers and I travel in darkness. It is certainly a different experience; travelling at speed through miles of tunnels, it is reminiscent of a fairground ride.

Eventually we arrive in Aberdeen, which is bathed in brilliant sunshine; it is certainly a contrast after the darkness of the train. I decide to stretch my legs and take a stroll after my long journey. Aberdeen seems a prosperous enough place. With all the usual shops it looks like any other U.K. town on a Saturday afternoon. Me, I hate all this shopping business. Retail therapy? Nightmare more like!

After an average Chinese meal, I wander over to the NorthLink terminal to wait for the Lerwick ferry. Here, whilst giving Ruth a call to update her on my progress, I notice a Shetland Island brochure and pick it up. It turns out that a Lifeboat Gala Day is held at Aith on the first Sunday in June. What luck, tomorrow is the first Sunday in June! As it is only about 20 miles from Lerwick to Aith, surely people will be driving there and will give me a lift? In addition, it could be a real chance to meet a man with a boat who can get me out to my three islands in that area.

The NorthLink ferry is a magnificent modern boat. It even has its own cinema, well more of a video, but then, who cares? We eventually leave Kirkwall around 11.30pm, next stop Lerwick and the Shetland Islands. I enjoy a couple of nips of Highland Park whisky before lying back in one of the comfortable, soft recliners to sleep. It has rained this evening, which I see as good news, as it should mean that there is less chance of it in the morning. What will happen tomorrow? I've really no idea, but I am feeling excited. It is a kind of nervous energy I suppose, rather like an athlete poised ready at the start of his race. I'm ready and looking forward to whatever lies ahead.

It is the D-Day anniversary. What would the boys have made of this boat? I clean myself up in the wonderful toilets on board; they will be the best I'll see for the next few weeks. Feeling much fresher, I take some breakfast and contemplate.

I decide to take a look out from the top deck and soon realise that I need my jacket! After all, it is 6.45am and we are in the North Sea off the Shetland Islands! Earlier I had woken in time to see the start of the Shetland Mainland opening up before me. It looked raw and exposed, undulating, although not too hilly; not a tree in sight with just a few small buildings, some sheep and nesting sea birds. But now I can see Bressay coming into view; it is one of my islands. It looks accessible enough and beyond to the right I can see the end of Noss.

But all that is in the future, for today it is to be Aith, from where I will try to get out to Linga, Papa Little and Vementry Island. How, what and when I still have to work out.

Bressay is to Lerwick what Kerrera is to Oban, a natural shelter for its harbour. A solitary puffin welcomes me onto the Shetland Mainland, my island number 16. I am close enough to the bird to get a really good view; what a great start. Lerwick looks a decent enough place but I am determined to leave it as soon as possible.

I change out of my jeans into my waterproof trousers, re-pack my kit, phone Ruth and then leave the ferry terminal.

After waiting for five minutes at the bus stop, a friendly local takes pity on me and gives me a lift. Evidently, I would have waited some time for a bus as today, being Sunday, there is no public transport! After calling at the local tip, the man kindly goes out of his way to drop me at Aith. It is only 9am, I have reached my destination and I have even been invited to a Midsummer Night party! What a shame that I will have returned home to York by then.

I sit around and wait. It's fascinating the people you meet if you sit long enough. Today it's the Coxon of the local Lifeboat and, amazingly, he has spent some time at Spurn Point. We have a yarn and he says that it will be no problem to get me out to the islands. So introductions are made, time passes but unfortunately no boat is forthcoming.

By 1pm, I decide to give up and leave Aith; I don't want to be around for the Gala. I decide to walk the four miles from Aith, along a minor road, which leads to the Salmon Farm, overlooking Vementry Island. Under normal circumstances, it would have been a moderate walk, but carrying a heavy pack, it is anything but. Eventually I reach the Salmon Farm where I get talking to a farmer. Here, at its nearest point, the island is only five to six metres off the mainland, but the water is too deep to wade across.

Unfortunately, the farmer's boat is not in working order. However, before too long, I meet a family, who say that they can take me over to the island for two hours. Now, if I were just ticking them off, I would have jumped at this opportunity. But, my dream is to sleep a night on each island, so that I can truly experience each one. I decline their offer.

However, it seems that all is not lost. There is a man working on the Salmon Farm below, he might be able to get me over. This also proves to be a non-starter. When I get talking to him he explains, "The work finishes today so I can't get you back in, in the morning."

Finally, with the farmer's permission, I put up my tent. Looking on the positive, it's a great site, soft grass, even ground, close to the sea, a water supply at the Salmon Farm, oystercatchers everywhere and fulmars nesting in front of me, just to my left. Nicely settled inside my tent, it's time to study my maps and make a new plan of attack. I am so drawn to these places. I just love these islands. I know Ruth would have loved it here too.

Ronald Regan died last night aged 93.

Refreshed after a good night's sleep, I look out of my tent. What a perfect location this is. But I need to get moving. After rolling my tent up in the Salmon Farmer's shed, I walk the four miles back to Aith. As I set off a swan comes to say "goodbye." My pack is weighing me down and I am feeling anything but fit.

By 7.45am, I arrive back in Aith and manage to meet the men that I need to speak to. "Yeah, we can get you out no problem, but the boat is broken." For me, this is just one too many "Yes but No's." The Lerwick bus leaves in five minutes, so I have no time to sit around. I catch it with not a moment to spare.

After stopping to pick up a few supplies in Lerwick, I catch another bus to Scalloway, the old capital, to try to get to Hildasay, Oxna and Papa. This area has a much more Scandinavian feel to it. In fact, the Shetland Islands certainly feels more Scandinavian than Scottish. Strangely enough, with wooden houses, quays, boats and little yachts everywhere, I cannot decide whether the Shetland Islands are rich or poor.

In Scalloway I find the Scottish Tourism sign "Boat Trips." "Brilliant," I think, but there is no one about.

Back at the pier, I am starting to feel that my island dream is just that. A dream. A dream, which will never get going. But what would I do without my islands? Whilst I am sitting there, a boatman suggests that I try Hamnavoe. "There are smaller boats there and it's near to Papa and Oxna." So I set out again. This time it's a four and a half mile walk to Hamnavoe.

Upon my arrival, I find that there are boats around, but no one to get me out. However, whilst there, I am educated by a ten-year-old boy, on the subject of crabs. He is inspirational. "This one is a Spider, this is a Green Back male, this is two years old, this one is 14 years old, bubbles mean it's breathing." His latest crab specimen, with one leg broken off, looks rather worse for wear. "It'll grow back", the boy says confidently. What knowledge for one so young, but I suppose that this is his life.

There is nothing left but to seek some solace in food and drink. So I purchase a few beers, a tin of sweetcorn and some blackbean sauce; the best I can do for a vegan banquet, before retiring to the other side of the bay to set up camp. My purchases provide a truly wonderful feast. Afterwards, as I sit applying cream to my sunburnt face, I reflect on how I can move forwards from here. Eventually, I decide that I will aim for Foula tomorrow, subject to buses and ferries.

I could have slept all day. I pack without breakfast; it's no problem I ate too much yesterday anyway. My face is burning.

I catch the bus to Lerwick; such is the landscape and the vegetation that it feels like I am travelling through the Yorkshire Dales. I just love it. Arriving in Lerwick, I phone to book my place on the Foula ferry.

Afterwards as I travel by bus to Walls, from where I am to catch the Foula ferry, I find myself in conversation with two drunks. Why do they always pick on me? It's certainly quite early in the day to be drunk. As I step off the bus, prepared to start my walk towards the ferry, a lady in a car is there to pick me up and drive me to it personally. What wonderful service.

The Foula ferry is not a big one. Already, by the time I arrive, a car has been lifted hydraulically onto the deck and now stands there, filling every last inch of space. It turns out that our Captain for the journey has been a Pilot at Spurn Point and still has a house in Willerby, Hull. What a small world.

It is about 14 miles to Foula, one of the most remote inhabited islands in Scotland. I am informed that on average around 60% of the passengers vomit on the journey across. Fortunately, one of the crew tells me, the seas are good today; which is a relief as my stomach is only just hanging onto its non-existent breakfast! Also, because the harbour is so exposed, the ferry will be hauled out of the sea on arrival at Foula.

As our boat starts to makes its approach, Foula, island number 17, rises imposingly out of the ocean. Foula meaning "Bird Island," has a population of 28 inhabitants.

Ham Voe, to the east of the island, provides the best that can be offered in terms of a harbour for Foula. As the ferry draws close, I notice at the top end of the quay, an old Lifeboat, resting there after its many years of faithful service as the island's ferry. Once I disembark, I stop to watch the car, which is hoisted off the ferry by the power driven crane; it is then followed by four bags of tarmac. Next, the ferry itself is plucked from the water, as effortlessly as one would pick up a toy boat, before it finally comes to rest, secure in its own stout concrete structure.

As I am marvelling at the wonders of such a feat, one of the islanders introduces herself, welcomes me to Foula and hands me some literature about the island. What a superb welcome, I am most impressed.

Taking her advice, I walk for about a mile in search of a suitable campsite at the south of the island. The sun is shining and I am so relieved to have finally set foot on one of my islands. On my left the road takes me past the island's airstrip. As I start to leave the road looking for somewhere suitable to pitch my tent, The Noup, a 248 metre crag rises distinctively to my left. I start to walk through The Daal; a valley which separates The Noup from the island's other peaks. It is awe inspiring. I am so busy looking around for the perfect site that suddenly, before I can do a thing about it, I feel my legs disappear beneath me and realise that I have walked into a bog!

Shit! So here I am, over 30kg on my back, an Ordnance Survey map in one hand, my walking stick in the other, my right leg completely lost to the top of my knee in a thick brown gunge and my left leg trapped to just below my knee. If this isn't bad enough, just as I am just starting to assess the situation, suddenly out of nowhere two, three, four, six ferocious giant birds swoop down in front of me, heading straight for my eyes. In the nick of time, instinctively, I raise my stick to protect my face and they soar back up into the air. Welcome to Foula!

As quickly as is humanly possibly, I use my only walking stick to lever myself out of the bog whilst at the same time trying to fend off my attackers with it. I heave a massive sigh of relief when I finally get beyond the war zone and the birds' interest in me ceases, leaving me free to set up my camp in peace.

After something to eat, I walk in an effort to dry myself out. Still looking out for the giant birds, I walk to the top of The Noup. From here, I can see far beyond the airstrip out towards the Shetland Mainland. I continue my walk visiting the old Kirk and the Lighthouse, at the southernmost tip of the island. But my heart is feeling heavy, why has this been such a difficult trip?

My feet and my boots are still soaking wet. I decide to keep walking and wander over towards the Airport. I am just strolling down the runway when I notice a car flashing its lights at me. It is one of the islanders, who thought I was someone else. We have a yarn and I learn that the giant birds are called Great Skuas or Bonxies. Evidently the island has the world's largest colony of them. Now he tells me! It seems that these giant birds will swoop menacingly even if they aren't defending their chicks, so my experience is not unusual for someone walking off track. *Without a doubt, Bonxies will become the thing I hate most about the islands, the bastards.*

I walk over to the Airport Terminal building to collect some water and, after waiting for an available line to become available, there only being a limited number on the island, I give Ruth a call. It's so nice to speak to her. Afterwards, I sit until the early hours watching some Shetland ponies, a stereotype image of the Shetland Islands. At 3am, it is still light.

I awake to bad weather. The weather is symptomatic of my mood; I am feeling very down. My feet, socks and boots are still wet through. The weather is shit, my dream is disappearing and I have little energy left.

At 1.00pm, Radio Scotland announces that the weather is improving towards the west. Naively I consider Foula to be West Scotland. However, there is West Scotland and then there is Foula! Based on this information, like a fool, I set out to walk up Hamnafield, a 344-metre peak which is currently shrouded in mist. Foolishly, I tell myself that by the time I have walked across the valley it will have lifted. What an idiot! This is a massive error of judgement. I end up getting lost in the mist and, after some time, start to panic when I realise that I have been going round in a small circle. I had never believed that this really happened to people, but now I know first hand that it is true. "Where am I?" I sit down on the damp ground; my heart is racing. A still small voice of reason starts to take control and reminds me that when I started out I had the sea to my left. O.K. so if I walk back with the sea to my right I should be alright? Yes, I'll be walking in the right direction, but whether I am going to be safe is another matter.

I am lost in the thickest of mists. My eyes cannot even see the sea. I am completely reliant on my ears to pick up the sounds far below me. In addition, to make matters even worse, each time I try to walk in line with the sea, I run out of land as the island curves back on itself. Time after time, I am forced to use my stick and my hands to claw my way upwards over wet, slippery grass and rock in search of safety, whilst the Foula sheep look down on me from above in amazement at my stupidity. Repeatedly, I find myself looking upwards at sheer cliffs, knowing that the only way forward is to go upwards. There is no way back and, if I slip, I face a certain death below.

Never, in my life, have I been so frightened. With each ascent, I know that my arms and legs are getting weaker. Gripped by the terror of my plight, time loses all significance as I am wrestling for my survival. I have absolutely no idea how long I have been stuck in this predicament, but it seems forever since I left my tent. Numbly, my tired eyes start to search ahead. Is that ground really a bit flatter? Anxiously, I peer into the distance and miraculously, the terrain starts to level out before me. I haven't a clue where I am, but I am so relieved to be walking on easier ground. Then, amazingly, suddenly arising out of the mist, just a few feet ahead of me, appears my tent!

I am beyond myself with exhaustion. As I finally stretch out, in the safety of my little canvas home, I gaze at my feet, which are soaking wet and itching, and I know that my island dream is finished.

Some time later, before I sleep, I ring Ruth. It is so good to hear her calm voice, the voice of normality, the voice of home. Mentally and physically I have absolutely nothing left.

I awake to clear blue skies and as I take down my tent, I realise that I am also dismantling my dream. It is over. Although I have the money and, to a certain extent the physical energy, mentally I cannot take it; nor can I see a way to ever get to all the remote uninhabited islands.

Once back in Lerwick, even the Indian and Chinese Restaurants are closed. Not even comfort food is available. I phone Ruth to let her know I am coming home. It is only a matter of days since my departure; she has no idea how low I am. I catch the 7pm ferry from Lerwick to Aberdeen. I have nothing left, not even tears.

My single train fare from Aberdeen to York is £80.50. For me it is the final insult. Just get me home and give me my life back.

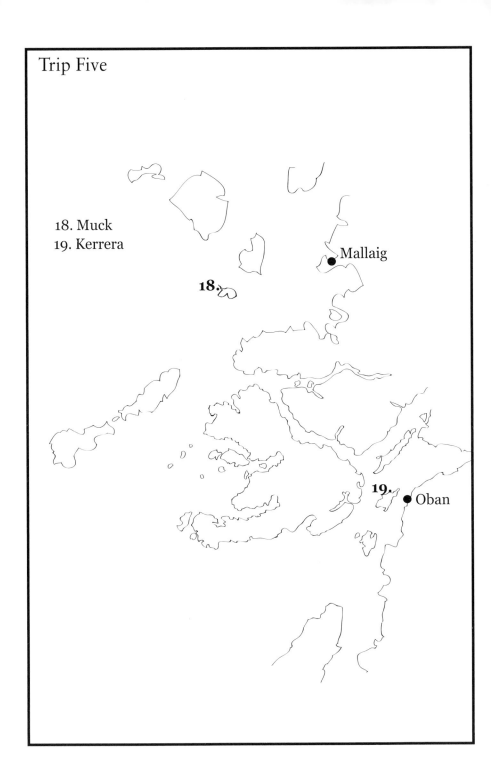

Trip Five

18. Muck
19. Kerrera

18.

19.

Mallaig

Oban

8
I'm Back!

It is exactly four months to the day since my dream died.

The Monday after I arrived back from the Shetland Islands, Donald Number One phoned to say he could get me out to the 11 islands around Barra. "Maybe next year" I said and he replied "No problem. Phone me."

The islands have refused to release their hold on me. I am back again to see if I can fulfil my dream. I realise that my main weakness has been in believing that I can turn up, talk to a man with a boat, and hey presto, I will be transported to the island of my dreams. Wrong! This trip is just to whet my appetite again and, if it goes to plan, I will come home and work out how I can get to all those countless uninhabited islands.

162 islands is a long way, but tomorrow I will sleep on number 21. One hurdle, one challenge at a time. My dream is no longer dead, may my journey continue.

This morning, my goodbye with Ruth is a beautiful long silent hug. Then we kiss each other and our rings. I can still taste her lipstick on my lips as the train leaves the station.

After changing trains in Edinburgh and Glasgow, I arrive once more in Mallaig. It is amazingly warm for the time of year. The Backpackers Hostel seems cleaner, fresher than before. I spend the night drinking my 16-year-old Highland Park whisky. I can now define bad whisky, although I still have to work out how good a good whisky is.

Awaking at 7.30am with a fuzzy head, a plate of Mexican chilli bean soup, some delicious German bread, washed down with a mug of coffee, seems to do the trick. As I look forward to getting some sea air in my lungs, I bid farewell to my fellow hostellers and head for the ferry terminal.

The new ferry is in for repairs, so today it is the smaller Staffa ferry which takes the three maintenance workers and myself over to Muck; my island number 18. Muck, the smallest of the Small Isles, is roughly two and a half miles wide and has a population of 35, including 11 children between the ages of one and ten. Their presence is an important ingredient for the healthy future of an island.

The ferry docks at Port Mor, to the south-east of the island. It is a beautiful little port with a handful of houses nestling close to the sea. Susan, who takes me along to the bunkhouse where I am staying for the next two nights, meets me off the ferry. I am bowled over by my new home. It is a simple tin and wood building, painted green and white, it sits on the roadside overlooking the harbour. Complete with a Rayburn fire, my double room costs the modest price of £10.50 per night. This bunkhouse can sleep up to eight people, but during my stay, I will have it all to myself. It is the perfect retreat.

It doesn't take me long to settle in, have a quick lunch and then get out and explore. I set off northwards along the only road on the island, passing on the way some beautiful Soay horses and a few sheep and cows. In the distance are views over to Rum, Eigg, and Canna. The outlines of each of these islands are so distinctive and happy memories of my earlier visit start flooding back.

Leaving the road, I continue to walk along the coastline. As I start climbing upwards, puffing and panting in the process, I realise just how unfit I have become. So I decide to give myself a rest. As I peer down onto the coastline below, I notice a white seal pup who appears to be washed up on the rocks below. At first, I think he has died, but then realise that he is just resting, as his parents appear back on the scene. All is well.

I walk on making a detour en route to climb to the top of Beinn Airein. At 137 metres, it is the islands' highest peak. Talk about out of condition! But I make it and am pleased that I have done so because the views out to Rum, Eigg, Canna, Skye and the mainland are a real joy.

On my way back I meet Rosie. She is my landlady; a lovely lady who is full of zest with a wonderful welcoming personality. She collects my two nights rent; £21 amazingly good value.

Having eaten, I give Ruth a call. I think that a telephone says such a lot about an island. The door to this one is kept shut by a rope. There is also a large stone wedged against it to make sure that it stays closed. Inside the box, protected from the elements, rests a brand new phone. A picture of the old and the new,

Muck certainly is making the best use of whatever it has.

It is now 7.30pm, time to read and enjoy a nip of malt. The electricity here is available between 8am and 11am and 5pm and 12.00 midnight. It is not a problem as I am already spoilt for amenities, having the use of a gas cooker and the kerosene Rayburn. On Muck, the islanders certainly make good use of each precious commodity. Recycling is another major success. Outside I empty my uncooked food into the bin marked "Rosie's Compost", whilst the cooked food goes into the one which says "John's Hens".

I sit and listen to the wind outside. Here, I am so content and snug in my island retreat.

I awake at 8am, looking through the open curtains onto the little harbour and the boats bobbing about in the water. What a start to the day, it really is the most perfect of settings.

After breakfast I explore to the east of Port Mor before looping back round onto the road again. Unfortunately, the Royal Air Force, who have decided to use the island as a flight path for their manoeuvres, temporarily disturb Muck's morning stillness and serenity. The real beauty of Muck is in its peace; it is serene in its calmness. I sit and stare out to sea. This is what I love so much about these islands. They calm me; offering me the chance to draw close to their soul, still my mind and become at one with them.

By the time I walk back to the bunkhouse, my stomach is telling me that it's lunchtime. I am just starting to enjoy a light snack when a visitor joins me; she is a lovely lady although going a little grey. Her name is Amy and she is a cross breed golden retriever. She is obviously at home here in the bunkhouse because she just walks in and stretches herself out contentedly in front of the Rayburn!

After lunch, my new companion and I take a stroll. It is a beautiful afternoon, the sun is shining and Amy bounds with energy. Never having been a dog lover before, for the first time I can see why people become so attached to them. Amy is a delight to be with. We sit and look out to sea as I enjoy a coffee from out of my flask.

Muck with its sense of community is a real success. I am sure that other islands have much to learn from her, for Muck has managed to bring young people together, which cannot have been easy. All the islands are different, yet this island seems to have embraced the good of the past with what is good from the present.

I love my journey around the islands, for each one is different, yet all of them are similar. I suppose that my journey to the uninhabited ones will be very different. I will just have to wait and see.

It is now 8.20pm. Everything is quiet, apart from the tick of the clock and the bubbling sound from the Rayburn. Amy is fast asleep in front of the fire. Rosie called in earlier for a yarn; she has lived on this island for 14 years. Amy, who is her dog, followed her home, but was back again, to rest in front of the Rayburn, half an hour later.

I awake to a most beautiful orange, blue and grey sky. Amy is curled up, fast asleep on the sofa. It is so strange, I am the most non-doggie person you could meet, yet I have loved having Amy around. Although I know that her life here on this island is a blessed one, somehow, I still feel responsible for her as she dozes away on the sofa.

It is time to pack, take breakfast and say farewell to the most perfect of hostels. I sit on the headland for my last hour and a half and Amy joins me. As we both stare out towards the sea and the sky, words like calm, still, and at one, inadequately describe the moment. But it is the best I can do. The ferry is appearing around the corner of Eigg and it is time for me to go.

As I get on the boat, some contractors are getting off. They are here to install Broadband on the island. At first, the slope down to the ferry proves too slippery and some sand has to be scattered, so that we can get onto the boat. Hopefully winter will kill off the green algae. Before this new pier was built, there was a debate over the location of it. The debate focussed on whether the pier should be put at the other side of the island, or erected at Port Mor where everything is centralised. The islanders opted for the latter, as they didn't want their island splitting. However, as the ferry has already been cancelled once this Autumn, due to the difficult approach in bad weather, it does make me question whether their final decision was the right one?

The ferry calls in at Eigg. It is great to be able to disembark and have a look at their new pier.

As the Small Isles fade in the distance and the port of Mallaig opens up before me once again, I begin to look forward to my return to Iona, tomorrow.

After a broken night's sleep at the Mallaig Youth Hostel, I arise at 4.30am and enjoy a cooked breakfast of lentils, potatoes, and vegemite, washed down by a cup of decaffeinated coffee, before I set off for the Railway Station. It is sad to be leaving Mallaig, which I find I am now enjoying in an abstract sort of way.

To my dismay, the Crianlarich train is starting to pull out of the station as I reach it. Thankfully, it is soon brought to a halt after the good-natured staff see me running along the platform, waving my walking stick ferociously in the air! It is only 6.00am and still dark. It feels just like one of my many early morning train journeys in India. Once aboard, I settle back into my seat and enjoy a quick snooze during the short rail journey to Crianlarich. Here I need to change trains and, because I face a three-quarter of an hour wait, I decide to call in at the small Station Café for an infusion of "real" coffee.

Inside, it is amusing to read the many signs requesting that luggage should not be left in the passageway, nor on the tables, nor in this or that particular area and to contemplate that instead perhaps I am required to place it on my head! But, apart from all the signs, it is a friendly enough place, a traditional down to earth café, with some lovely staff serving excellent coffee.

The journey onwards towards Oban is my most enjoyable ever. As I look out of my window, my eyes feast on the palette of natural colours lying amongst a rainbow, some lochs, mountains and the beautiful blanket of autumn leaves.

It is so good to return to Oban, the gateway to my islands. As I look out from the top deck of the Mull ferry, I am reminded of my first trip there. I was so excited. Yes, I am still excited on this journey, but as I watch my fellow passengers, I realise that this time I am feeling different, more confident I suppose.

My bus journey across Mull, towards the Iona ferry, passes without incident, as I enjoy the beautiful scenery on display. Mull is such a powerful, mountainous island although I must admit that my preference is towards the smaller ones. Although I have visited Iona before, I feel that I need to pay it another visit. Last time I was here, I was only passing through and on this occasion, I am keen to spend more time on the island.

As I leave the Iona ferry, I follow the road north to Lagandorain, where the Hostel is located. I am surprised to find that the building is full of people. It appears that a magic show is about to start. Malcolm Russell, a magician and physical comic, who is paying a visit to each inhabited island, is about to give a performance.

After the show is over, I am keen to talk to him and hear more about his journey. It seems that his interest in the islands is more of a backdrop to promoting his business. But, for me, to spend so much energy, time, and money in visiting such beautiful and remote islands, and then quite often only stay two hours, I find difficult to understand. The second thing that I question is around the ongoing discussion of "What is an island?" Some of the "islands" that Malcolm has visited he has walked to. Now, I find a lot of specialist field discussions quite ridiculous at times. For me an island is "a piece of land, surrounded by sea, that you can't walk to." It's as simple as that. What about "inland islands?" Scotland's mainland has countless rivers, streams and ditches all crossing over each other. How many "inland islands" are thus created!

However, saying all this, we all see things differently and I think he deserves to be applauded on three counts. Firstly, people are enjoying it; secondly it is raising the awareness of these beautiful islands and thirdly, Malcolm himself is sure to have an amazing experience.

I contemplate his challenge and realise that it is not difficult. If a place is inhabited, then by that very fact, it is also relatively accessible. If not, no one would be living there. For me, the real challenge is to get to the uninhabited islands. Most of these were inhabited in the past, but now, quite often, they are abandoned because of the difficulties in reaching them. Having said all this I have not yet managed to visit one uninhabited island, so perhaps I am just all talk, like so many people. Only time will tell.

My full weekend stay on Iona, three nights in total, is spent visiting Columba Bay, (the place where St. Columba landed and ultimately changed Iona forever,) eating, drinking at the Bar, and generally observing the other visitors.

For the majority of people who visit, Iona is their introduction to small islands. Indeed, for most of them it will be the smallest island that they will ever visit. Many of these visitors believe Iona possesses a special feel. This I agree with, yet I also believe that the smaller the island you visit the more heightened is that feeling. It is not solely because of Columba but because it is a small island. If you consider the numerous religious places that exist around the world, you will recognise that each possesses its own special feel. This feeling I am sure would be enhanced on a remote island.

Many people believe that Iona is the place where Columba first brought Christianity to the Britain. This is not true. St Brendan landed on Eileach an Naoimh, a small island in the Garvellachs, in the Firth of Lorn, prior to this. In fact, his monastery was founded there, 21 years before St Columba landed on Iona.

Many of Iona's visitors are day-trippers who arrive on organised coach trips. Undoubtedly, their visit to the island will be spiritually more uplifting than an average coach journey. Yet, amongst some of the visitors I am aware of an under current of self-righteousness. We are perfect, we are right, let's be nice to everyone. I find this so artificial.

I recognise that my time on Iona is complete. It is not for me. So, I catch the first ferry of the morning back over to Mull. From Fionnphort the early morning bus to Craignure connects me with the Oban ferry.

Arriving back in Oban, I enjoy a lunch at Tesco's before travelling by taxi to the Kerrera jetty, which is a mile and a half out of Oban at Gallanach. From here, all I have to do is signal the ferryman, by turning the Kerrera Ferry board over onto its black side. It is such a simple, clever system. Today I am not alone on the ferry journey across. Five other passengers and their dog accompany me. The dog is not at all sure about the boat and various tactics are used to encourage her aboard, coaxing, pleading, bribery by chocolate. Eventually the ferryman just grabs her by the back of the neck, hauls her onto the boat and then we are off! The small ferry certainly can motor and in less than five minutes, we are across the Sound of Kerrera and landing on my island number 19.

Kerrera, with its population of 30 inhabitants is about ten miles square in size. Being such a long island, it provides Oban Harbour with a natural shelter from the Firth of Lorn.

As I start to walk towards Lower Gylen at the south of the island, I am thinking to myself that Kerrera seems to be a slice of mainland Scotland lost in a time warp. However, it has a decent semi-circular road by island standards. There is such a lot for me to take in as I walk towards the Bunkhouse where I am staying; some high hills to my right, heather, brambles, telephone and electric cables, streams, gates across the road, sheep and boats on the water.

The heavens open as I am on my way. But, being reasonably protected by my decent outdoor clothing, I find it more of a pleasure than a hindrance. I have come to recognise that the wind and rain blowing down the hills is as much a part of these islands as is the sheep, the sea and the malt whisky.

Eventually I reach the Bunkhouse, which is a converted stable. Compact and on two levels, it is run by Andy and Jo, a lovely couple from Sussex, who have only just opened for business on 1st October. The more I let the surroundings soak into me, the more I realise just how ideal it is. O.K. so the toilet is outside and there is no shower, but for me it is the perfect place to stay for a while.

I love the sound of silence. All I can hear is the wind outside and the tick of the wall clock. The clock reminds me of childhood visits to my Grandparents; they would have loved these islands. All my forefathers were from the land but I took up a trade. It was seen as a step up.

Yet, even though I have taken a trade, I am being drawn to the land. I know my Grandfathers would have approved. They would have loved to swap places with me; but realistically they could never have hoped to have the time and money available to do what I am doing. I am in such a fortunate position, especially when I consider my roots. I never really knew my Grandfathers; after all, I was only 11 when the last one died. I feel a little sad about this, but I am sure they would have been proud of me.

The day is complete. Outside the rain descends in torrents; cascading onto the hills of Kerrera and bouncing against the Bunkhouse's small six-pane window. This Bunkhouse is so me; it reminds me of my room at home which is like a monk's cell. This room is small but adequate; material possessions mean nothing to me.

I don't see my island journey as a solitary one. I see it as something for both Ruth and I to share. Why my island journey is for the both of us is not fully clear to me yet, although I know that it will be revealed. I know that Ruth has to complete her own journey, to do the things that she wants and needs to do; and she will. The thought of all this makes me smile. I am blessed to have Ruth as my wife, my friend, and my confidante.

If I do complete the 162 islands, my main wish is that I remain humble.

The new day has made no difference to the rain. It is still pissing it down. Good old Radio Scotland says it is with us all day. I am sorry, but I cannot forget putting my faith in you on Foula! But, alright, for the moment it's the outdoor gear, so let's go for it!

I follow the road round to the west of the island; it would be a wonderful walk if it wasn't for the weather. The road is a four-wheel drive track in places. In other places, made significantly worse by all the rain, it certainly is no better than a trial bike circuit. But I press on. I have a go at taking a few pictures, but it really is hopeless as my viewfinder keeps getting misted over.

Eventually I reach the north of the island and as I turn to face Oban, Kerrera in an instant stops being an island. With a big city in touching distance, it becomes ugly and unappealing from my image of what an island should be. Undoubtedly it has its own beauty, but it is no longer secluded and private. Here Kerrera is exposed to the world of speed and noise, the world of western civilisation. It has lost its' "islandness".

At the north end of the island, is a monument to David Hutcheson, one of the founders of the Caledonian MacBrayne ferry service. It stands at the head of Oban Bay, a fitting reminder to each ferry as it sails in and out of the port.

I continue onwards, passing through a few farmyards along the way. As I shut each gate, making sure that none of the peacocks, ducks or Highland cattle escape, I breathe in the rawness of the farmyard with its distinctive cow smell. How I love this smell; it is the smell of my youth and now it is the smell of my islands.

Beyond here, at Ardantrive Bay, is a boat yard. As I walk back towards the road the rain starts to come down with a vengeance. I am fortunate though because, just as the heavens threaten to do their worst, I come across a small cave in which I can shelter. Within its safe confines, I am busy contemplating how caves like this one would have been used by the early islanders, when a Cal Mac ferry sails past me, taking yet another ferry load of memories back to the mainland.

I decide that Kerrera must have the most gates across roads of any island. I am most relieved to finally reach the road, where my mood lifts once again. The islands and especially the weather certainly do take your mind to extremes. Back on a decent road, I soon reach Lower Gylen and the Bunkhouse, where once again I have the place to myself. I find this hard to understand; the accommodation on the islands is so empty. I know that the North Americans are here in large numbers, but where are the British?

My evening is spent in solitude. I am happy to be alone with my thoughts and a bottle of malt. The rain laden heavens have now disappeared; replaced instead by thousands of stars which illuminate the clearest of skies. The vastness and beauty of our world never ceases to humble and inspire me. Lost amongst its beauty and majesty, I am aware how small I am in the greatness that we call earth.

Fortunately, the new day is dry with intermittent sunshine, which I definitely appreciate after yesterday's downpours. I decide to wander over to Gylen Castle, a 16th century Clan McDougall stronghold at the south of the island, which is not far from where I am staying. I know Ruth would be interested to see it, having relatives with the same name. On my way there, I meet two Scottish Natural Heritage members who tell me that there are many important fossils in the area. Sadly, as with many things, it seems that people are destroying the country's legacy and removing them for their own pleasure.

Gylen Castle stands majestically looking out towards Bach Island, Mull, and the Firth of Lorn. It is slowly being restored for all of its visitors to enjoy. As I walk around the base of the castle I spot my first mink. It looks like a ferret, only stockier with a beautiful black coat.

The coastline on this part of the island is truly amazing. I am not a geologist, just someone who loves island coastlines, but even with my limited knowledge, the rock formation here seems most unusual. The best way I can describe it is that it has a look of solid concrete, interspersed with pebbles and boulders. Initially as I scale down the rocks, closer to the sea, I presume that it is part of the castle's foundations, but then realise that it is actually part of the island's rock formation.

Now, it is time to head back to the Bunkhouse passing some wild goats along the way. My stay on Kerrera is almost at an end. I have loved the remote part of the island but hated the north end, violated by the intrusion of Oban and the boatyard.

After an uncomfortable night's sleep, I awake to more wind and rain. A Geordie, who agrees with my opinions about Kerrera, joins me on the short ferry ride back to the mainland, and gives me a lift into town. It is so good to check back into the Youth Hostel. Having gone three days without a shower, I cannot wait to get clean again. Looking and feeling much fresher, I head into town for some food and a few beers.

My head is full of thoughts about the future. I think I will take my car with me on my next trip; it will mean that I can be more flexible and it certainly will be less hard work. But how will I cope with all the driving, and what will it cost to take my car everywhere? My sleep on this trip has been terrible, so maybe I could take in a few B&B's next time, or perhaps I could just sleep in the car? I will have to check it all out.

After eight pints, I stagger back to the Hostel and fall into bed. I am so tired.

Definitely feeling worse for wear, I awake from my drunken sleep, pack my kit and head into town. What a wind! It is so strong that I am in danger of being blown into the middle of the road, as I walk from the Youth Hostel towards the Railway Station where I will catch my train back to York. My head is pounding and I am feeling shattered. However, I feel that my island journey is possible, as long as my physical and mental health holds, the work and money continues to come in, and Ruth and I can make it happen together. After all that, I guess it is just down to contacts, the weather and God.

Now, it is time to head south, back to my wife and my home. It is time to re-group and to plan. I will be back again in Spring. It was a shame about the Shetland episode earlier this year, but I have learnt a lot from the experience, my confidence is growing and I am looking forward to the journey ahead.

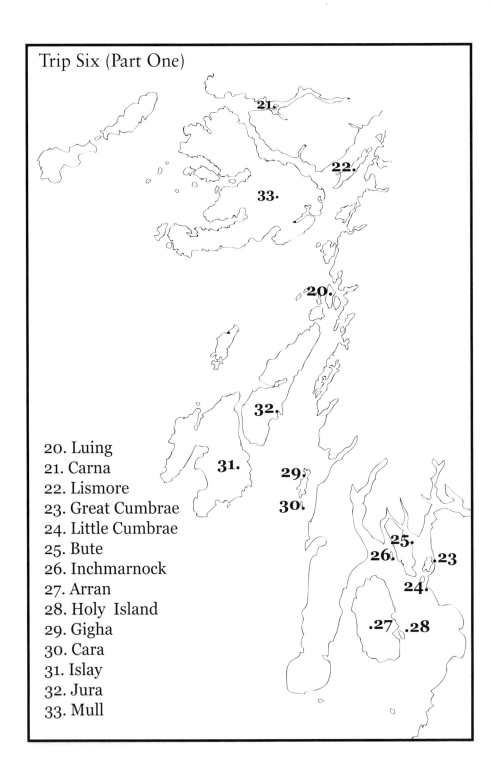

Trip Six (Part One)

20. Luing
21. Carna
22. Lismore
23. Great Cumbrae
24. Little Cumbrae
25. Bute
26. Inchmarnock
27. Arran
28. Holy Island
29. Gigha
30. Cara
31. Islay
32. Jura
33. Mull

9

THE ROAD TRIP – PART ONE

TUESDAY 22ND MARCH 2005
TO SATURDAY 9TH APRIL 2005

It is March 2005 and my year has been a full one already.

During the winter, I recognised how important sleep is. Without it, I become groggy and grumpy. I am also aware that I need to be focussed and well organised if I am to achieve my dream.

In addition, I acknowledge that I need to have contacts in place before I leave home for my island visits. Whilst on the Shetland Islands trip, I lost my drive and my passion and I became demoralised. Therefore, time spent at my desk is far more important than I had previously realised. I need to allow myself time to research and contact boatmen and make my plans. Even then, once everything is in place, I may still get out onto the road and find that my plans have disintegrated. If they do, at least it will be because of things that are out of my control, such as my health or the weather.

On my Shetland Islands trip, I ended up feeling like a beggar. "Please give me a lift, please can you take me to that island, please can I put my tent up here?" I have learnt such a lot from that experience which has helped me mould my plans for the future.

I now have boatmen in place for about ten uninhabited islands. I haven't found it that easy from an ethical point of view, as I've never been one for cold calling; it's just not me. I've really had to push myself to cold call on the boatmen. Anyway, I've done it, so, all I need now is a bit of luck.

Another big change on this trip is that I am going to take my car with me. I recognise now that it is impossible to try and do this journey on public transport.

As far as sleeping alone on an uninhabited island, I must admit that I find the thought a little eerie. But, I'm sure I'll be fine, although I imagine the nights will be something of an experience.

Three months ago, the Asian Tsunami took place. The news hit the British media around lunchtime on Boxing Day, only four days before Ruth and I were due to leave for a holiday in Thailand. Over 200,000 people were killed in its wake. We decided to go ahead with our travels, avoiding the parts physically affected by the Tsunami. But it has certainly made me sit up and think about the magnitude of what I am trying to do. The power of the sea in its wildest form should never be underestimated.

I am also taking with me on this trip, a CD by Donald McNeill from Colonsay. One day I hope to meet him, I find his singing inspirational. His music takes me to the very heart of island life, highlighting many of the social issues, which most islanders face each day.

I think of my humble beginnings and see my life unfolding. I know that the only thing that will stop it developing to a level beyond my current thinking, are my thoughts themselves. I know that thoughts create my future.

I have decided to call this stage of my journey "The Road Trip". It is the changeover from public transport to the luxury of having a private vehicle.

Yet, as with all human beings, there is always that little niggling thought at the back of your mind. "You never know if what you choose to do in life is the best choice". With my island journey, I can only hope that it is.

At 6.30pm last night, Ruth and I decided that I should leave this morning. It was a day earlier than planned. But we both knew that the timing was right, my car was packed and my island feet were itching to go. So, after a last minute run around followed by some quiet time together, the lights were out by 9.30pm.

As always, due to the childlike excitement I experience in such situations, I am awake at 1.00am. So, I decide to get up and within an hour and a half, Ruth is waving me goodbye. Driving at this time in the morning certainly has its advantages. The only other people travelling are lorry drivers, instead of being surrounded by crazy young executives rushing up the motorway towards their next appointment.

With all the kit I am carrying on this trip, I can be self-contained for more than two weeks. It certainly is a good move bringing my car, the volume of kit has amazed me.

I have always had this image of being a hobo, as the Americans call them, just hitting the road with a small travel bag, no cares in the world and a life unfolding before me. However, romanticism is one thing and realism is another. So I am happy to be a classy hobo with a car!

This is the first time that I've driven through Glasgow on my own. Not being the most confident of drivers, especially in the big city, I am relieved to see it disappear into my rear view mirror. I arrive at Tyndrum by 8.20am where I fill up with fuel and take a coffee. Whilst I am sitting in the car, enjoying my warm drink, I watch two backpackers struggling with their kit. Having been in the same position on most of my earlier trips, I feel for them. This time, I have brought with me four times the amount that they are carrying. Maybe they are happy to carry all their kit, but it's not for me.

I feel like a King, as I finally pull away in my car, my own self-contained little unit. It is going to be great having it with me, as I travel to my islands. Tyndrum has certainly proved to be a thought provoking coffee stop. Location wise it is a major crossover point. Behind me, the south and Glasgow have gone. In front of me, the islands are almost on the horizon. I realise that I see the UK in three sections; south of Yorkshire you can forget about it; Yorkshire to Glasgow is a buffer zone; North of Glasgow, civilisation.

My journey to Oban is just the best. With my window wide open, the heating on full blast, my woolly hat to keep my hair in check and Donald singing his heart out, it cannot get much better.

Viewing Oban from the top of the hill, it all seems surreal. Below me, the town unfolds, but my eyes are drawn to the Cal Mac ferries, which are ready to sail out to my glorious islands. Once in the town, I visit the Cal Mac terminal to check out some details. A new building is in the process of being built, to replace the old terminal. Business is definitely looking good.

Today, I am not travelling on one of their ferries. Instead, I am heading northwards where I will take a council run ferry to Luing, island number 20.

En route, I spend a little time on Seil, which used to be an island, before the introduction of a bridge changed things. Spanning across the Clachan Sound, a stream, which later flows into the Atlantic, it certainly is a clever piece of marketing to name it the "Bridge over the Atlantic." At its highest point, the hump is so steep that I am unable to see over the bonnet of my car, let alone view anything coming in the opposite direction. The bridge reminds me of a

1970's fireplace, with two circular alcoves either side of "the fire!"

At Ellanbeich, which is the main village on Seil, I am amazed to find a hive of tourist activity. I love the terraced dormer bungalows, built of slate and meticulously white washed, with a barrel outside each one to catch the rainwater. I am also interested to read more about the history of the slate islands Luing, Seil, and Easdale. Easdale is an island below 40 hectares; it is also the most populated Scottish island below 40 hectares. One day I'll visit it, but for now, I have more than enough to excite me.

Whilst I wait for the Luing ferry I stop to use the toilet and am introduced to my first experience of "sensor lighting." What a brilliant idea!

My excitement mounts as I join the council ferry for the short crossing to Luing. Soon it will be getting dark. To get your car on and off the ferry, you are required to drive onto it at one corner and then leave from it at the diagonally opposite corner. Skilfully, the ferryman in his yellow waterproofs, manages to squeeze a handful of cars on; there is not an inch to spare. The crossing is calm and, in less than five minutes, I am on Luing. How would I have ever done this on public transport? I am so lucky.

The ferry docks at the north end of the island. Around the ferry terminal area are toilets, a waiting room, and a few houses. I decide to take a quick blast across the island, to have a look around before night falls. Six by one and a half miles in area, Luing has a reasonable sized population of 220 people.

As I drive away from the ferry terminal, the terrain starts to become steeper; either side of the road is heavy rough grazing land. The Luing cows, a special breed to the island, are a deep reddish brown colour; they are powerful and compact animals. At one point two calfs, with their mothers, block the narrow road ahead.

Beyond me, the road starts to open up into perfect, fertile green pasture. I drive over to Black Mill Bay, on the west side of the island, and, from here watch the powerful waves in the Sound of Luing crash against the rocks.

My hotel for the night is just beyond the main village of Cullipool. I decide to park up in a disused slate quarry below Cnoc Dhomhnuill, which at 94 metres is the highest point on the island. It is an awesome setting. I am on cloud nine. This morning I awoke in my bed in Yorkshire and tonight I will sleep in a disused slate mine on an island in Scotland. How amazing can life be?

I cook my food on my gas stove in a small hole of slate. From here, I can see Garbh, Naoimh, Dubh Mor, and Fladda lighthouse; the first three are islands that I will soon be visiting. This has got to be the best place I will ever find to sleep.

It is very windy and it starts to rain. But, to enhance such a wonderful setting I open one of my 40th birthday presents, from Ruth. It is a miniature bottle of 23-year-old Highland Park whisky. Later, I lower my passenger seat and sleep contentedly.

Heaven is a slate mine on Luing Island.

I awake around 4.30am after managing six hours sleep. It is an improvement on the previous nights three and a half. During the night, each time I awoke, I could see the beam of light from Fladda Lighthouse shining brightly across the water.

I am amused to hear BBC Radio Scotland's weather gem for the day, "more organised rain." Left, right, left, right, quick march! It could only happen in Scotland!

After my first night's sleep in the car, I realise how much of an upheaval it creates. I drive back towards the north of the island and park outside the new Fire Station. Here I am able to reorganise my bedroom-cum passenger seat and boot, before cooking myself some breakfast. My breakfast of bread, peanut butter, vegan sausages, orange juice, and coffee is so healthy it is almost depressing. Still it tastes good. It has been a great start to life in my car. I loved parking up last night, putting my head down, and then awaking this morning to such solitude. I love that "on the road" feeling.

Feeling a bit more organised, I go to the pay phone, near the ferry terminal, and phone Ruth. It only costs 30 pence for a 15-minute call, good old BT; you can keep your expensive mobile phones! Whilst we are chatting, I become aware of a Luing style traffic jam, six cars all racing to get onto the first ferry. Barely batting an eyelid, the ferryman expertly navigates all of them on board. Moments later, packed like a tin of sardines, the full ferry slowly manoeuvres its way across the Cuan Sound towards Seil.

After a hectic morning rush hour, I drive southwards to visit the old Church and graveyard, which overlooks Shuna Sound and the island of Shuna. All around Luing are the islands that I hope to visit later on this trip. As I enter the immaculately maintained graveyard, the sun squeezes itself through the dark rain clouds overhead, and shines brightly onto the waters of the Shuna Sound. The graveyard is possibly the tidiest I've ever seen.

The grave of Albert Sultcs, a Latvian seaman, jumps out at me as I wander amongst its manicured grounds. He died in the waters off Luing in 1936. His fellow seamen are also lying here in adjoining graves. On Albert's gravestone, I look at the picture of a young, smartly dressed, man. He seems so out of place against the backdrop of this small island graveyard.

Nearby is the hamlet of Toberonochy, with its bay, not full of sand and pebbles but of slate. Even the walls of the local houses and the benches are made of slate. The island of Luing is certainly unique. It will be interesting how I will see it, after I have experienced other islands.

Next to the Village Hall in Cullipool, I stop to pay a visit to the toilets; outside I notice five crushed frogs.

I have enjoyed my visit to Luing. The islanders have plans to turn it into a trust, similar to the ones on Eigg and Gigha. I think that Luing has a very healthy future ahead.

Later, as I am enjoying my lunch, back in Oban, I overhear the following conversation, "I don't like to pay for anything in advance because if you die you don't get your money back." Is that right?!

Yesterday, I realised that I had a spare day, because I'm not booked onto the Lismore ferry until Friday. So after looking at my maps and making a few phone calls, I decide to pay a visit to Carna, off the Ardnamurchan peninsula. I am unable to organise transport only to Carna, but am offered a cottage for the night, with free transport included, so I decide to go for it.

After my lunch, I set off on the long drive to Ardnamurchan Point, the most westerly point in the U.K., and finally arrive there ten minutes before the sun sets. My eyes are tired, due to the strong spring sunshine, which has accompanied me throughout the last two hours of my journey. The road to the Point is extremely isolated and for much of the way only a single track.

The sunset is not the best I have ever seen, but the views across to Rum and Eigg more than compensate for this. As I leave Ardnamurchan, the lights on the lighthouse start to shine across the ever-darkening sky. Wearily I follow the road back towards Glenborrodale, my jump off point for Carna in the morning. Carna will be the smallest island that I have visited so far, less than a quarter the size of Iona.

With only nine and a half hours sleep in the last two days, plus all my driving today, physically I am shattered. So, I find a quiet place to park up for the night and settle down for my second night in the car. I love it.

After a great night's sleep, I am awake by 6.00am. Outside, overnight there has been heavy rain and my car windows have all steamed up. The news, emitting from my car radio, announces that today 50 % of the children in the Western Isles are off school with flu, and that early morning rain will soon clear from the west. As I couldn't be in a more westerly position this is good news.

I give Ruth an early morning call and make my way back to Glenborrodale to meet Andy from Ardnamurchan Charters. He is going to get me over to Carna and will also give me the keys for the cottage. I am really looking forward to it all, although I am not expecting too much of the accommodation, which has certainly blown a hole in my budget.

It is only 8.45am when I arrive, a little earlier than planned, but Andy and his lovely wife Allison make me very welcome. "Would you like some tea?" As I respond in the affirmative, a piping hot mug of tea appears, followed by a yarn which continues until Andy's son arrives and it is time for us to leave.

Prompted by Andy, I jump into an inflatable boat, which is then lowered, assisted by a tractor and trailer, into the water. Once afloat, we speed towards deeper water where we transfer onto a larger boat. This is the one that takes us over to Carna.

For me, all this is so exciting. Once we have docked, I climb from the boat onto a pontoon, made from parts of an old fish farm. It bounces up and down as I walk towards the island. To my left I can see an old wooden pontoon, now abandoned and rotting away. In front of me is my cottage.

I am pleasantly surprised. It is a large, white washed, bungalow with yellow doors. Seemingly, parts of the building date as far back as the 17th century. It's hard to believe that this will be all mine for the duration of my stay. Alongside stands a modern farm building, where the generator, which provides electricity for my cottage and another one, is stored; both cottages are available to rent from the island owner.

Andy opens the door to the cottage and leads me inside. Pointing towards the large kitchen window, overlooking the water outside, he tells me that from here you can regularly spot otters. The cottage is great. There are clean sheets, duvet, a real fire, and a nice large bath.

Carna is the smallest island that I have visited so far and, at island number 21 it is the first one that doesn't have a full time population. Tonight a couple will arrive to stay in the second of the two cottages, but, for now, I have the whole island to myself. Knowing this leaves me in a state of excitement, a combination of delight and awe.

Most of all, I feel peaceful. It's amazing how life's thoughts and plans can suddenly become meaningless. As I stand here in this cottage kitchen, with all my food supplies spread out on the table before me, I feel overwhelmed knowing that all these islands still lie ahead of me, each one waiting to share its own scenic beauty, tranquillity and soul. I am so lucky to be starting on such a journey. How can such a simple man as myself be so blessed?

I look out of the window. The rain is lifting, the sky is grey with a hint of sunshine, life cannot get much better. Now I know why I left a day early, for today is my reward.

I watch as Andy, who is also the caretaker of the island, and his son Tom, leave the pontoon and climb onto their boat. Waving me goodbye, I am left alone on an island. It is a magical feeling.

I have certainly changed over the last few years. Now, here on Carna, I have found a place where I belong. Tucked away, amongst the remoteness of Ardnamurchan, I have found my peace, my life. It is like awaking from a deep sleep. I know that these islands will become my life.

I have some breakfast, and then set off for a walk around the island. Andy mentioned that the island needs some work doing on the drainage. Seeing how wet it is, this is an understatement. The island has a slightly abandoned feel to it. I wonder if all the non-scheduled ferry islands are like this? I will try to build up my knowledge and develop a feel for all of the islands. At the moment, not one person exists who can talk about them all because nobody has ever experienced them all. I find this an amazing thought.

By the time I am out of the village area, I start to realise that there is no path. I find myself wading through heather, literally beating my way up to get to the peak.

The highest point of the island is Cruachan Charna; at 169 metres, the summit is really windy. Perhaps I'm naive, but I had never realised that the higher you go the windier it becomes. As I look out towards Ardnamurchan, the sea appears relatively calm, but up here the wind is immense. I take a photo of Clyde and head slowly back down to the village.

All around I notice abandoned implements rusting away in the long grass. It's hard to imagine that not so long ago this land was fertile and worked. Then I glimpse two large dollops of frog's spawn and remember my school dinners. "Pass the jam!"

The light is fading fast. As the sun drops on the horizon, its rays briefly illuminate the dark water, only to be swiftly extinguished by a group of fast moving clouds.

Safely home for the night, I find that although the generator works, the electric does not. So, I spend my evening relaxing and enjoying the magical glow of candles and a beautiful coal fire.

It has been a wonderful day in the Ardnamurchan wilderness.

Today is only my fourth day on the road, although it feels as though I have been away much longer. I slept reasonably well last night until 2.30am but after that it was hit and miss. For some strange reason, I locked the cottage doors before I went to sleep. Definitely a touch of mainland mentality on my part. OK so in the other cottage a couple had arrived late yesterday afternoon. But, why did I need to lock the door?

After breakfast I have a hot bath before leaving the cottage, I've no idea when I'll get my next chance to be clean.

The morning is overcast, yet dry. I take my kit and my rubbish to the end of the pontoon and wait for Andy. The water is serenely still. Disappointingly, I have not seen a single otter, although there have been plenty of other things for me to assimilate during my stay. I try to weigh up all of my experiences, which is difficult as I have little to compare them with. It is sad to be leaving Carna, but I am looking forward to the prospect of many other wonderful islands, which still await me.

On our trip back to the mainland, Andy mentions that he also does a ferry service to the Small Isles. Part of his cargo today is a bag of dead fish for a lady's cat on Muck. I think to myself what a charmed life Andy and the cat have.

Once back on terra firma and reunited with my car, I head towards Oban. My journey is broken to stop at the supermarket in Fort William, where I stock up on a few supplies and have a bite to eat. My God, I am completely unprepared for the noise, the people and the hassle. Please get me out of here! I am amazed at the shock to my senses after just one night of solitude.

Today I am going over to Lismore, which sits in Loch Linnhe, to the north-east of Oban. As I arrive at Oban ferry terminal, an hour before departure, I watch in amazement at the "gold rush" to Mull. There are so many islands, yet only about half a dozen of them seem to be well known. Today it takes two ferries to cope with the tourist demand for Mull.

Now, let me get this right, this is relaxation? One car, one husband travelling with one wife, with a towel over her head, two children, four bicycles on roof rack, one dog, and one trailer weighed down with over spilling luggage. It is no wonder that the UK has such a long hour's work culture. After this holiday the poor guy definitely needs to go back to work for a rest.

Eventually, it is time for the Lismore ferry to depart from a small adjoining slipway. The island has a population of 145 people and it will be my island number 22. We are all required to reverse onto the boat and yours truly is the last one to do so. I have to admit here and now that this is the first time I have ever reversed onto a ferry. In fact, now I come to think about it, it is only the second ferry I have ever driven onto in a car. So, you've got the picture. With three cars, a four-wheel drive vehicle, plus a large builder's merchant lorry with trailer, the ferry is tight for space.

"Do I need to go further on?"
"No if you're not far enough back the door will push you on."
"Oh right."

I am a little twitchy to say the least, but these lads seem to know what they are doing. Once onboard, with fortunately no damage to my car, we set off on our 50-minute crossing. It's a pleasant journey with people on the ferry chatting to one another. The glorious weather, accompanied by the lightest of breezes, helps to create a most enjoyable and relaxed atmosphere during our short passage to

Lismore.

The ferry arrives at Achnacroish, mid way down the island's south-east coast. Evidently, there is also a second ferry, which carries passengers from the north-east corner of Lismore across to the mainland. Many of the islanders use this ferry to commute for their daily work, choosing to leave their cars on the mainland. Upon my arrival, I phone Ruth, and then look at my map to get my bearings. Lismore has a good feel to it.

Having checked the map, I decide to drive first to the top of the island, and then explore in a southerly direction, in the hope that I will later get to see the sun set in the south-west. The island is around ten miles in length and only about a mile and a half at its widest point. There is an excellent road, which runs the full length of the island.

At the most northern tip, where the water is crystal clear, I enjoy fantastic views northwards over to Shuna, an island which is further up Loch Linnhe. For both car drivers and cyclists alike, Lismore is a dream of an island with roads that are both flat and empty. These, surrounded by lush grass, a land that is fertile with not too much heather, trees and wonderful buildings, all help to contribute towards the overall feeling of an all round perfect island.

Port Ramsay, where the island's northern ferry terminal is situated, has a lovely traditional feel to it. In addition to the pier, it also boasts a row of small terraced bungalows, which look seawards, separated from their traditional stone walled gardens, by a road. It feels just like a place my Grandfathers could have walked up to, scraped the dirt off their boots, on the dirt scrapers outside the doors, and gone inside. In front of the bungalows, a small stream meanders into a muddy bay, a mixture of mud, pebbles and sand, it is an ideal setting for birdlife.

As I make my way south again, I come off the main road onto a smaller track. Along here I stop, from time to time, to open a gate or two until eventually I reach Tirefour Castle, well, its ruins actually. I am popping with excitement as I run up the grassy hill towards the remains of the Castle. I am not disappointed, for, from the top are views east, across the silken waters of the Lynn of Lorn, to the very small island Eilean Dubh. You never know what you are going to find. Here on Lismore it seems that around every corner lies something new, tucked away amongst the peace and solitude of this beautiful island.

Later, I pause to watch a couple of stationary cows. They stare back at me, their outlines silhouetted in front of some tired stone outbuildings, each poorly covered by a rusty old corrugated roof. Although my journey is to visit and sleep on all of these islands, my dream is much bigger than that. It is to promote them to more people. I want to encourage others to visit or live on them. These islands need new people if they are to survive. They need an income, a livelihood for those who choose or are chosen to live here. Farming is finished, but tourism is a seasonal business and a shop window to attract alternative business.

Further south is a reconstructed croft house. These traditional croft houses seem to be an attraction for some people. As an uninhabited building, from my perspective it is just a living museum. Surely, the money could have been used in a better way? I cannot understand why people are impressed to invest so much in the past with so little regard for the future. But then, I don't have a great interest in buildings and history. I place a greater value on the present.

The road ends in a mud track and, unless I want to get stuck, it is time to acknowledge that I drive a basic Skoda, not a 4 x 4!

Fortunately, I am just in time to watch a perfect sunset over the south-west of the island. Beyond my horizon are Ardnamurchan and Carna. It has been another amazing day.

The night starts to chill, so I return to the passenger ferry terminal and park for the night. As the last ferry passenger disembarks, I pull up my mud-splattered car, roll down my passenger seat and draw a close to the day.

After seven and a half hours of glorious sleep, I awake at 5.30am, relaxed and rejuvenated, to the sight of the sun rising over the mainland; a fusion of magnificent colours. Now, it is time for my morning duties, some breakfast, and then a phone call to Ruth.

I am booked on the 7.50am Port Ramsay ferry to Oban. On my way back north towards the ferry terminal, I stop to visit the island graveyard. Here, I am observed by a splendid male peacock, perched on the surrounding stone wall. He brings back happy memories of the peacocks that I saw in Rajasthan, India, and their wonderful early morning calls.

I look over towards my dirt covered car. You would think that I have been rallying. Well, I suppose I have. Whilst waiting for the ferry to arrive, I carry out an obligatory car cum home spring clean. Eventually the ferry appears and as it pulls in, the island post van drives to the end of the pier to exchange the outgoing post for the incoming mail.

I am the second car onto the ferry. Leaving Lismore's coastline for deeper waters, I become spellbound by the perfect sea state, which surrounds us this morning. Not only is it perfect, it is also unreal, embellished by what I can only describe as Andy Warhol style swirls.

Before very long I am back in Oban, ready to start a long drive south. Today I am heading for Largs, on the River Clyde, from where I will sail to Great Cumbrae, my island number 23.

As I reach Tyndrum, there is a lot of traffic going northbound. It is the Easter weekend and travelling around Loch Lomond is extremely slow, with everyone driving bumper to bumper.

Driving down the Clyde estuary quite saddens me. Once home to so many of the big shipbuilding companies, today only a few now remain, leaving behind a state of dereliction. I know that changing times are a fact of life, but somehow it doesn't seem right to have taken all that work away from the working man.

From Largs, my ferry crossing is a very quick ten minutes in the rain. Great Cumbrae's hey day was at the peak of the Clyde shipbuilding industry. On days like today the island still sees many visitors, but cheap air travel and the promise of better weather has meant that others now choose to fly overseas for their summer holidays.

The island is like Amsterdam, a cyclists' heaven. Around it is a 12-mile circular, flat, road, with four places where you can hire bicycles of all sizes, and even trailers for the little ones. Today, the main centre of Millport, with my first views across to Little Cumbrae, is a hive of traditional British seaside resort activity. Little Cumbrae itself sits alluringly across the Tan, a stretch of water which divides the two islands. Compared to Millport today, it looks a serene, peaceful location.

Driving around the circular road it is amusing to watch the various cycling techniques. A wobble starting at the bike hire shop, which continues all the way down the middle of the road, translates into "It's a long time since I've been on a bike!" A red-faced cyclist, half way around the island, rolling from side to side on his seat means, "I'm so out of condition. I don't think this was a very good idea after all!" Hey, no worries guys, the Pubs will still be open by the time you make it back to Millport!

After cruising around the island, I start to like Great Cumbrae, in an abstract sort of way. It has no pretensions. It is what it is and always has been, a place where you can escape the chaos of city life and breathe in some fresh, invigorating sea air.

I make my phone calls and start to look for a place to park up for the night. On Great Cumbrae, signs state that camping is not allowed. The Scottish Outdoor Access Code was introduced last month, so now, realistically camping has to be permitted as long as it is carried out responsibly. But, even before the law changed, would sleeping in my car have been classed as camping? I love just parking up and bedding down.

Tonight, I park right at the top of the island, off the main road, down a small track. Here high upon Barbay Hill, at 127 metres, I can see Largs in the distance, in the opposite direction Little Cumbrae and, to my right, the Isle of Bute. Whilst being able to observe the world, at the same time I am away from it. I love that feeling.

Tonight Scotland are playing Italy, in a World Cup qualifying match in Milan, and although they play well, they lose 2-0. Scottish pride in football is a form of national identity. Yes, they are 88th in the world but the "Tartan Army" still manages to take 10,000 fans to Italy.

After another good night's sleep in my car, I awake to a distinct nip in the air. Being at the highest point on the island is one reason for this, but also last night the clocks went forward. I am glad to jump back into my car and take the short drive into Millport, where I park up the car and re-arrange my kit. Today I am going over to Little Cumbrae, my island number 24. I give Cumbrae Voyages, who are taking me out there, a call and am told to be at the pier by 11.40am.

This is good news as it means that I have time for a coffee, washed down by a beer, after which I go over to the pier and wait. It is absolutely bloody freezing. At 12.25pm, I decide to phone again. It seems that there has been a slight mix up; they thought that I was in Largs. "No worries, we'll see you in five minutes".

Ten minutes later, a RIB (rigid inflatable boat) roars towards the pier. It is a real man's piece of kit, the biggest RIB that I have ever seen. The power of it is awesome, definitely white-knuckle stuff. Cumbrae Voyages, as well as doing charter work, also do tourist trips, so with me today are four other people. Our journey involves a wonderful tour around the Little Cumbrae coast, also far in the distance I can see Ailsa Craig.

As we pull into Little Cumbrae's small pier, I get a delightful surprise when I look up and see a castle to my right and Little Cumbrae House to my left. Preferring not to spoil the visual impact of an island by looking at pictures in advance of a trip, this scene is well worth the wait.

Little Cumbrae House, a splendid 49 roomed regal looking building, is surrounded by beautifully manicured lawns, in the middle of which the Scottish flag proudly flies from its flagpole. It is good to have arrived. I am met at the pier by Alistair and Bonnie, the island caretakers. They are a couple in their late forties, who both appear completely at ease in these isolated surroundings.

After a quick introduction, the RIB departs and we make our way over towards my campsite. Campsite? At the side of the house is a perfectly maintained lawn, where I am to put my tent! It is five star accommodation! I am still recovering from the shock when I am told the rate; £5 to land and £1.50 to camp. This has got to be the bargain of the year. I leave my pack on the lawn and follow them into the house, where I am advised that I also have use of a toilet and shower. What great facilities.

Next, I am treated to a guided tour of the workshop. Al is certainly well organised and efficient. You could say boys and their toys, but, without doubt, there is also a strong work ethic here. Numerous islands have caretakers in place, but to find a couple who are so conscientious and motivated has got to be the making of an island.

Beyond the workshop is Al and Bonnie's cottage. Kindly they invite me in for a coffee, and before we realise it, a couple of hours have passed in an instant. But, as they have their family visiting and I have an island to explore, I decline a second mug of coffee and agree to meet up with them all later. Helpfully, just as I am leaving, they give me a fantastic map of the island and advise me where best to walk.

The work on Al and Bonnie's own cottage is to a very high standard. Although Al has trade experience, to me it is his overriding love and devotion for this island, which surpasses all of that. At the moment, they are working on the big house, all 49 rooms, and the work they have done there so far is first class. The island owner is a sensible man, leaving things in Al and Bonnie's capable hands. Although my experience is only limited, I am most impressed to see how well the island is managed. Here, a perfect union between owner and caretaker has resulted in the island flourishing.

My walkabout takes me over to a lighthouse, which is three quarters of a mile across the island on the west coast. Like so many others, it is now automated. I am amazed by the standard of the accommodation, which is extremely well maintained. However, the same cannot be said for the adjacent rail track, which drops steeply down towards the sea. Formerly, it was used to bring up supplies from the sea, but now it is rusting away and is non-existent in places.

Slowly, I take the steep walk back up the hill to the island's highest point. At 123 metres the old lighthouse ruin still remains, at a place, which is named, surprise, surprise, Lighthouse Hill. Today there are the remnants of a solid stone building, which had no windows or doors, only openings, and on it, you can still see the inscription from the Clyde Lighthouse Trust, which dates the building between 1756 and 1956.

As I look slightly ahead, towards a plateau of land, I notice the sky is heavy with gulls, gliding comfortably in the breeze. They remind me of snowflakes at the height of a snowstorm. Around this island, the paths have been kept cut back, trees planted and pheasants fed. It will be interesting to compare it with Sanda Island, which I am due to visit later on this trip.

Reaching the most northerly tip of the island, Sheenawally Point, across the Tan I can see Great Cumbrae and the "big city" of Millport, gleaming in the sunshine. It all seems a world away. Yet, bizarrely from here, I can almost see my car.

Little Cumbrae is really a beautiful island; it is a wonderful example of nature and man living comfortably together. As I wander back from the old lighthouse, dotted around the lochs in large yellow clusters, the spring daffodils sway in the breeze, protected from damage by stronger, sturdier bushes.

Reaching the pier on the east of the island, as the tide is out, I wander over to neighbouring Castle Island to take a closer look at its square tower castle. I am amazed to see how solid it still is, impressively so, for a derelict building. Certainly none of your modern building techniques were used here. At the top of the tower, I am rewarded with some great views of Little Cumbrae House, the buildings, my campsite and the Scottish flag. Without doubt, Little Cumbrae is an extraordinary island, remarkable by its excellent condition and house, which is undeniably majestic.

I spend the evening socialising with Al, Bonnie and their family. It is a great night, listening to music, drinking whisky, and playing pool on the red covered pool table. As I settle down for the night, I reflect what a wonderful day I have had, on this fantastic island, amongst such genuine people. I feel so fortunate to have been able to share this experience.

After a noisy night under canvas, disturbed by the sounds of geese, ducks, wind and heavy rain, I finally awaken at 8.30am. It has been my first night under canvas on this trip. I pack away my kit, and then roll up my tent in the entrance of the big house. I am really sorry to be saying farewell to Little Cumbrae. As I wait at the pier with my kit, Al comes to say goodbye; three of his family are also leaving today.

At 11.00am, the RIB arrives and, after putting on waterproofs, we set off at a break neck speed.......for Largs! This is until I hold up my arm and the RIB comes to an abrupt halt.

"Great Cumbrae?"

I shout in the affirmative and the vessel corrects its course, after which we aim for Great Cumbrae. I knew that there was something wrong when, in line with Farland Point, Millport Bay was fast disappearing from view!

Great Cumbrae has grown on me. After dumping my kit in the car, I head for some lunch at the Ritz Café. What a great name, It is a wonderful place, 1950's in style, very traditional, completely set in a time warp, but in the most positive of ways. To me, you can keep your fast food outlets, just come to the Ritz Café, Great Cumbrae.

My choice off the menu? Peas, yep, just that! A large plate of peas, with vinegar, washed down with a mug of black coffee. Result? One happy, traditional vegan Yorkshireman.

After catching the ferry back to Largs, I drive north to Wemyss Bay, for a 35-minute crossing to Rothesay, Isle of Bute, my island number 25. At Wemyss Bay, I easily board the Bute ferry. It is empty, but a big queue is waiting on the island itself for those holidaymakers who are returning to the mainland. Today is the end of the Bank Holiday weekend, and, in addition, a wet day, the worst of this trip. But, after a week on the road, I can't complain.

As I drive off the ferry, Bute strikes me as similar to Great Cumbrae, yet with a more affluent feel, although we're still talking a 1950's seaside resort.

After visiting the Tourist Information Centre and stocking up on food, I decide to drive over to the west coast. Bute is a large island, the 11th biggest of the 162. Really, for me it is too big, although it is starting to grow on me.

As I look across St. Ninian's Bay, I get my first view of Inchmarnock. It looks beautiful, only 60 metres high, it is about two miles long by half a mile wide. To me it is certainly a special island, one which I am looking forward to with great anticipation. For, if things go to plan, Inchmarnock will be the first uninhabited island that I will ever sleep on. I gaze across the water, wondering what it will feel like to sleep there, all on my own.

All these islands are becoming special to me. Even Bute has its own beauty. I am so lucky to have retained my childlike sense of wonder, of awe. The islands, especially the smaller ones, are all individuals, each with their own soul. Spurred on by my childlike exuberance, I drive down a pot-holed track towards, what I believe is the slipway which will get me to Inchmarnock. But, at the end, it is deserted and there is nobody to be seen.

I drive back up the slipway, and head northwards to Ettrick Bay, a beautiful quiet spot, which has the most idyllic of views down the Kyles of Bute. Tonight this will be the view from my apartment.

After I have parked up my car, I sit, just relaxing, watching the various ducks, waders and oystercatchers which frequent the coastal rock pools. Time stands still as I rest, only distracted by the beauty all around me. I don't know how long I have been sitting there, when my stomach starts to tell me it is hungry and I realise that daylight is fading fast.

After a meal, my hunger satisfied, I open Ruth's Easter card and treat myself to the vegan chocolate egg that she gave me before I left home. It is a real score and Clyde enjoys a piece too.

I am awake at 6.30am. As I have arrived on Bute a day earlier than planned, it is likely that today I will be going for a swim. For me, a swim means a shower, teeth clean, hair wash and blow dry, normal ablutions which, when living on an island are not always easy to achieve.

I drive down to the slipway for Inchmarnock around 7.30am. There is not a soul to be seen. Eventually, around 9.00am, a man appears at the next house and suggests that I phone Jock, the man who will get me to the island, as usually he is here before now. I leave a message on Jock's answer machine and head for the big city of Rothesay.

I decide to stop off for some food at a place called Café Zavaroni, and am enjoying a lively banter with everyone, when suddenly, with a loud clunk, the penny drops. Just a minute, that name, Zavaroni. Yep, it is the family of Lena, from "Opportunity Knocks" fame in the early 1970's. I remember her well; she was a big issue for me at the time, Lena being ten and me being only nine. I had one massive crush on her but the problem was the age difference. You see, a year is a big difference when you are only nine; a major problem, older women and all that. Ah well, great memories.

After I leave the café, I stop off to pay a visit to the public toilets. Rothesay's Victorian toilets should never be used as toilets; they are a museum. Somehow, it just doesn't feel right to use them for a piss. Built in 1899 for only £5 and then renovated in the 1990s for £300,000, the interior is magnificent with walls and floors covered entirely in decorative ceramic tiles. The whole place sparkles; they are the best public toilets in Scotland.

Today Rothesay is bubbling with animated conversation about Charles and Camilla, due to the announcement that Camilla is to become the Duchess of Rothesay.

I buy a newspaper and then phone my answer machine. Jock will meet me in the morning at 8.00am. What a prompt response. I suppose no more than I should expect. Word, locally, is that the owners of Inchmarnock are very well respected people in these parts.

So, it is Plan B, the swimming pool. It is so nice to be clean. I am a light sleeper and much prefer my car to a hotel, but, being dirty is a challenge for me, as normally I like to have two showers a day. After the "swim, I take a little snooze, a siesta in my car. Tonight I will park up in the same place as last night.

Everything is so still here. Yes, it's windy, but the stillness is the soul of nature all around you. If you allow yourself to sink into it, stillness is the catalyst to being at one with yourself and all that which surrounds you, just like meditating.

The islands are slowly starting to unfold and I begin to realise that they are waiting for me. Bute is wonderful on this cold spring day. Each year 1,000,000 visitors come here.

I bed down for the night, in my hotel on wheels, drifting off in nervous anticipation of Inchmarnock, waiting for me in the morning. Eight days, six in my car; how I love it, especially after my shower.

I awake to a very cold Argyll morning. Dressed only in my knickers, tee shirt and trainers, I try to organise myself as best as I can. First job, out of the car for a piss. The steam rises as the yellow liquid hits the frozen ground. I hastily tuck my bits back into my knickers, and then dive into the boot for my trousers and walking boots. What a sight I must look!

Now, as you are all aware, normally bodily functions don't just end there. So, on my way to the slip for Inchmarnock, needs must and I stop off in a wood to go for a "sit down." It's a wonderful thing to do in the fresh open air, even though it is a bit cool on the nether regions this morning. A little hole is dug, and then covered up, and so nature is back to nature.

At the slip, Ian, Jock's employee, is the first to appear. He is a tall, solidly built man with a wonderful, no nonsense approach to life. Owing to the cold weather, the inflatable, which is to be used to get me over to Inchmarnock, island number 26, needs pumping up this morning.

Ten minutes later Jock, a clean-shaven, solid, good-looking man, arrives. I like him immediately; he is a man's man, a decent guy who would be as comfortable fronting a board meeting as working over on the island.

Ian suggests that I wear my wellies to get out of the boat onto Inchmarnock. This proves to be great advice. After yarning for a while, we make our way across the green algae covered slip, taking care not to slip in the process, and from here take the short crossing to my first ever uninhabited island. It seems so strange because, although no one lives on Inchmarnock, this morning it is a hive of activity. My expectations of an uninhabited island are of no people. Maybe some of them are like that, but I suppose all of them must have human voices competing with the sounds of nature from time to time?

As we approach the island, I notice a large JCB with tank style tracks, in front of a considerable size modern farm building. We make our way over to the building, which houses a selection of standard farm equipment; two tractors, a trailer, two quad bikes, a caravan and a table and chair for coffee and lunch breaks. The caravan, parked in the corner of the building, is there in case it is impossible to make the one-mile journey across Inchmarnock Sound back to

Bute after a day's work. Although Inchmarnock is a relatively sheltered island, it can quickly become cut off, in bad weather.

There is no mains electric on the island and when it is needed, it is supplied by a generator. I am fascinated to learn that this building has been used for a Hen Night! That's real women for you. But your thoughts have got to be with the poor male stripper. I don't know about shrinking, more like vanishing in this biting cold weather!

"Coffee and lunch breaks are at 10.00 and 12.00 join us if you'd like" Jock announces.

Before then it is time to go walkabout. I notice that the quads have permanent gloves fitted; to me this is a clue. Ian's advice about wearing wellies turns out to be the advice of the day. The track is water logged and boggy. Even one of the organic highland cattle on the island has managed to get bogged down, stuck in the mud up to the top of its legs. What magnificent beasts they are. As they stare in my direction through their profusion of long shaggy fringes, I contemplate how important their thick coats must be, in helping them to withstand such harsh conditions.

The buildings of St. Marnoc's Chapel, Midpark and Southpark all come in quick succession. Midpark is a derelict, traditional farmhouse. Its walls are all still standing although most of its roofs have caved in. Recently, it looks as though Jock and Ian have fitted new wooden gates, to prevent the cattle from wandering amongst the derelict buildings. Prior to the present owners, this island was not well maintained and there are areas towards the southern part where wild briars are particularly widespread. Inchmarnock is now farmed as an organic farm, therefore no chemicals are used and these briars will have to be controlled through hard work alone.

Towards the south-east, the briars intermingle with patches of woodland. After I manage to extricate myself from them, I arrive upon a small bay, which is at the end of the island. I feel just like an explorer, it is a great feeling. Here, the rocks are lying diagonally on top of one another and, next to them lies a small gravel beach; a welcome retreat to the multitude of herring gulls, oystercatchers and cormorants.

At the most southerly point of the island I come across two caves. They are smaller than the ones on Eigg, but they are more rustic and exciting. Although I have no knowledge of geology, I love looking at all these different rock formations. The diversity around the islands is immense. Purely based on the islands I have experienced so far, the potential for visitors with an interest in specialist fields is unlimited. Myself, I am not a specialist in anything, but I love the "over-all-ness" of it all. I can understand why so many of these islands were called "Priest Island". For to find God through nature, there can be no better place.

As I walk up the west coast, I am amazed how wet it all is. Of course, having no experience of uninhabited islands, maybe this is just normal?

I stroll towards the peak of the island. In the distance, I notice more highland cows watching me. Some of them are brown coated and some are black, they stand motionless. Silhouetted against the grey skies I notice their strong curved horns. At the centre of the island, after all the briars, rock and wet ground, I am surprised to come across a freshly ploughed field. If I had not explored this island fully, I would never have come across this, and would never have witnessed first hand the hard work that Ian and Jock are putting in on Inchmarnock. For me, this only serves to reinforce my goal of staying overnight on all these islands. By doing what I am doing, I have the time to explore and see each island in different weathers, and understand how and where each island changes in the shortest of distances.

As I reach the top, 60 metres above sea level, the strong wind hits me. From here, the island looks very different from its southern coastline. Here it appears fertile and well drained.

But now it is time for lunch and a yarn after which I will make my way down to the north end of the island. Walking back towards the farm building, I notice bomb craters dotted around. This island was evacuated during the Second World War and used for bombing practice.

After lunch, my first stop is Northpark, near the top of the island. I stop to take a closer look at it. It is certainly is a thought provoking place. The roof seems to have only caved in recently. Inside the rooms, I can still see beds, cupboards, books, copies of "Reader's Digest" and even wallpaper remaining on the walls. It is the most recently abandoned house on the islands that I have seen so far. The wallpaper is maybe 20 years old, but it still brings a sense of the past. Inchmarnock, like Little Cumbrae is in safe hands. The past has gone and we need to live in the present. Yes, we can all learn from the past, but we mustn't let our thoughts become clouded by romantic notions of these now uninhabited islands. They are uninhabited because life became too difficult, often impossible for their inhabitants. Yes, let your minds wander, but then take a reality check, could you really live in such locations?

Inchmarnock is still divided into its three original farms, but farmed as one. It has 180 highland cattle and grows organic turnip. The land around Northpark is fertile pasture. Here 50 or so of the cattle decide to come and say "Hello." They associate humans with bringing food and yes, I have come from a farming background. But, 50 powerful beasts, many with strong horns, running towards you, well that's another thing. Apprehensive is one word, twitchy is another. But I don't stop around to deliberate, instead I leg it fast!

After stopping for my afternoon coffee break, I visit St. Marnoc's Chapel. Inchmarnock means Island of Marnoc. Now all that remains of St. Marnoc's Chapel these days is a few stones. Archaeologists have been, and removed their "finds," i.e. the bones. Today what remains are very striking, coffin sized holes all around.

Once again back at the farm building, I chat to Jock about how cold it is. We both agree that people must have been really hardy to have lived on this island. As I watch Ian and himself leave the island for the night, I contemplate, "Tonight, this will be the very first island that I have ever slept on all by myself."

This thought starts to sit quite naturally and normally with me as I wander back inside the farm building, my five star hotel for the night. Very kindly Jock has said to use the caravan, the President's Suite, if I want to. So, after enjoying a little whisky and listening to some radio, I go to sleep.

After a reasonable night's sleep, I awake at 6.00am. I must admit that it did feel a bit eerie last night. It was a cold rough night, and going to the toilet in the darkness on an uninhabited island, does get the mind going. Inside the caravan was no problem, but going into a large dark farm building was eerie. Once I was outside and going to the "toilet" then I was fine. Its' funny but, I seem to sleep better in places most people would prefer not to sleep in! Take last night for instance, and then in my car. Yet put me in a nice hotel and I struggle to sleep. Strange....

I awake and watch the sunrise over Bute. Once up, I take a trip down to the low tide, below the seaweed line, where I lower my trousers and squat, enjoying the views of Bute and the fresh air around my nether regions. I just love using the sea for my morning visits; it is so natural and invigorating.
Jock and Ian arrive just after 8.00am and comment how fresh I am looking. As

Ian jumps out of the boat onto the island, I jump back in and Jock takes me over to Bute.

I am just walking back along the slip, over the wet green algae when, yes, down I go onto my arse, leaving both my jacket and pack a wet, green colour. A real Inchmarnock souvenir!

I thank Jock for all his help and he wishes me all the best for my adventures. As I shake his hand, it is as I first thought; I've met a really decent man, a true gent. For me this is a picture that is starting to build. The image of a Scotsman being tight couldn't be further away from the truth. All I am experiencing is kindness and generosity.

As I get back into my car, I can best describe it as going from the Artic to the Tropics. I am so pleased to thaw out once I get the car heater blasting away. It has been bitterly cold on Inchmarnock.

I stop off for a bite to eat, in Rothesay, and then queue up for the ferry back to the mainland. I am first in the queue. Behind me, an elegant looking lady pulls up in her car. "Were you the man who spent the night on Inchmarnock last night?" she asks. I quickly start to rack my brain, who on earth would know that I had spent the night there? It's Jock's wife! I guess with my open boot, all the outdoor kit in March, and my ponytail, I have given away a few clues. What a lovely lady, and what a small world.

I arrive in Wemyss Bay and drive directly south to Adrossan, where I take the ferry to Brodick, Arran, and my island number 27. I must say that outside on the deck I get some questioning looks as I walk around in a tee shirt, whilst everyone else is wrapped up in their thick sweaters and jackets. But after Inchmarnock, this feels like summer to me!

Arran is a major holiday resort. I would guess that it must be the most visited holiday island in Scotland. To me it feels like the mainland. The larger, especially tourist islands hold little appeal for me. It is not what I am about. But hey, different islands for different people, its just that my favourites are the smaller, wilder ones.

I transfer my visit to Holy Island from Saturday to Friday, so hopefully I'll be able to get onto Gigha on Saturday. Although everything is planned, things are always in constant flux, and to keep abreast of it all is quite an ongoing challenge in itself.

After making all my phone calls, I drive south to Lamlash where I get my first views of Holy Island. Part covered in mist, I feel quite excited. I look back towards Lamlash, with all its smart houses, shops and restaurants and look forward to my journey to Holy Island tomorrow.

I follow the road around the island to Lochranza in the north. Arran is an island of contrasts, mountainous in the north, with a lovely coastline covering the southern, more populated, part of the island. Yet generally, to me it is unappealing. At Lochranza, I note that the Claonaig ferry seems to take 12 to 15 cars. I hope that I will manage to get onto the ferry on Saturday for my trip to Gigha. But, I'm sure it will be O.K. This trip does seem to be green lights at every turn.

The circuit around Arran is 55 miles, with numerous tourist attractions en route. At the north end of the island, I park, briefly, near Lochranza Castle, yes it's majestic, but it doesn't appeal to me. I end the day curled up in my sleeping bag inside the car, parked up in a relatively quiet location. But, before I go to sleep, I finish off the bottle of Highland Park, which I started on Luing. What restraint.

After a good night's sleep, I give Ruth an early morning phone call. Today is her first day back at work after a three-month sabbatical. It will be strange not to be able to phone her whenever I wish. I guess that makes me feel even more isolated up here.

After enjoying my breakfast, with Lochranza Castle in the background and oystercatchers to my right, I head for the Arran Distillery. It is the newest whisky distillery in Scotland, starting in 1995. I enjoy the tour, which is very interesting, if a little above my head at times. I have to say, I do feel a bit like a "hillbilly" in the big city. Here I am dressed in my island gear, whilst everyone else on the tour is walking around in immaculate clothing with perfectly groomed hair!

The Arran Whisky is so young that it tastes green. Still, I buy a couple of miniatures just to give it the benefit of the doubt!

Arran has a strange feel to it. I think it's the volume of holiday homes here, supposedly over 50%. Because it is so accessible for Glasgow, it is the easiest thing for people to pop over on the ferry. You don't get a feel of islanders here; instead, it is of wall-to-wall tourists.

The morning is a mixture of mist and rain; it makes me wonder if the crossing to Holy Island will take place today. I don't need to worry; the boat to Holy Island leaves Lamlash at 2.45pm as planned. Holy Island is the site of a centre for World Peace and Health and today a yoga course begins on the island. So over 30 people, 29 women and just one token male are also travelling there with me. Each boat holds only ten people, and I am in the last boat going over.

Arriving on Holy Island, my island number 28, immediately my eyes are drawn to eight Buddhist stupas on my right, and a renovated farmhouse in front of me. The farmhouse appears to have been completed to a good standard, with cream coloured cement rendered walls and red paintwork. It houses many bedrooms, a dining hall and an adjoining hall.

After a friendly welcome from my hosts, I pay my dues for the night, and head to my room to settle in, leaving the yoga group to enjoy their chatter. The residents here seem down to earth, friendly and sincere with it.

At 5.00pm, I decide to join a handful of Buddhists, in a separate building, for their evening prayer and meditation, after which it is time for my evening meal of vegan soup and bread. The soup is adequate, but the bread is fantastic. It is warm and wholesome and oozes a wonderful homemade taste. As no alcohol is permitted on the island, I wash all this down with some water and a banana.

I make up my mind that I am going to get up early in the morning and explore the island, so before long I am tucked up in bed and fast asleep. Being a morning person, this suits me fine, meaning that, just as day starts to break at 6.30am, I am already on my way, having enjoyed a quick slice of toast and a cup of coffee.

On Holy Island you are asked not to walk in certain places. The steep cliffs on the east side of the island, with no recognised path, are considered too dangerous for visitors to walk on. Although I wonder if this applies more to the yoga course visitors, my respect for all of these islands is of paramount importance, and I heed the request.

I take the short walk to the north end of the island. To my left Lamlash Bay is calm and peaceful, it is a beautiful tranquil morning. Like myself, the day is still awaking and some of the island's feral goats come to say "Hello," they appear to be quite used to human contact.

I am only just starting to get into my stride when the track ends and it is time to turn back towards the farmhouse. On the other side of the farmhouse is an old boathouse, which now houses a Buddhist temple, a gompa, on the upper floor and an unofficial café on the ground level.

The path along the west coast of the island overlooks Lamlash Bay and Arran; it is well maintained and easily walkable. Occasionally a Buddhist mural, painted onto the side of some of the large rocks, seems to leap out at you from amongst the greenery. With their bright colours and Tibetan icons, they look so out of place in this calm and beautiful environment.

After a short while, gradually awakening out of the morning mist, and towering above me to my left I see Mullach Mor. At 314 metres, it is the highest point of the island. I stare upwards and notice the sheep with their lambs grazing, searching for today's breakfast, whilst some more goats look down at me from their magnificent mountain panorama.

Here St. Mo Las Cave is open to the elements. Inside, the ground is two feet lower than outside. It is a place of history of that there is no doubt, but it holds little interest for me, in comparison to all the beauty that surrounds it. But then, hey I'm not a historian.

The island's first lighthouse, at the south-western corner of the island, is being used for a female retreat. I understand that they have already been in retreat for two and a half years; it is a three and a half year retreat. I am always impressed at people's devotion and belief. I wish I had such. One day I hope to sit on top of a hill, or live alone on a barren island, for a month. The recluse, the hermit in me is always coming to the surface. But for now, I admire those who engage in what I can only aspire to.

The second lighthouse at Pillar Rock Point to the south-east of the island, is in excellent decorative condition.

By the time I arrive back at the farmhouse, everyone is up and about, so I join them all in a little breakfast. Then after a yarn with some of the residents, it is time for me to say my farewells. Holy Island, now safely in the hands of Samye Ling Buddhists is a great example of the potential for these islands. The isolated islands of Scotland have yet to be fully appreciated for the diversity that they offer.

It is late morning when the boat for Arran leaves Holy Island. It is a strange D.I.Y. affair. All the boatmen still seem to be learning how to manoeuvre it in and out of the jetty.

Knowing that the Lochranza to Claonaig (Kintyre) ferry was cancelled yesterday, because of mechanical problems, I arrive in good time for the 1.30pm ferry, only to join the queue of people who have been waiting patiently for it since 8.30am. Fortunately, a replacement ferry is on its way. When the ferry finally arrives, it is only able to take 12 cars, and so two are left at Lochranza. Apparently, one of those left behind had actually arrived at 9.00am but went for a bite to eat, thus losing his precious place in the queue.

Onboard the ferry are two female hitchhikers. "Are you going to......?" "No."

Upon landing, I make the short trip from Claonaig, southwards along the Kintyre peninsula to Tayinloan, where I am to catch the ferry to Gigha, my island number 29. It is through flat, fertile green land, so different from much of the Scotland that I have seen before. My 20-minute crossing to Ardiminish is over a calm, velvet sea. With the sun shining, the sky a shimmering blue, and a gentle soothing breeze on my face, life does not get much better.

Gigha is the most perfect, car-ferried island that I have yet to see. The best way that I can describe the island is to say that it is "normal." What a great word. By normal, I mean that it has not been taken over by holiday homes, like islands such as Arran. The islanders themselves own the island. The people of Gigha are an every day group of hard working, decent people.

Employment is spread over numerous businesses. The ferry itself employs a reasonable number of the islanders and some low cost housing is in the process of being built. All in all the future of Gigha is looking very healthy. The most striking thing about Gigha is its volume of piers, slips and jetties, in addition to around 20 mooring points in Ardminish Bay where yachts can anchor. This place is a heaven for yachties!

I park up for the night at Port Mor, to the north of the island. From here I watch another spectacular sunset, which I am able to enjoy all to myself. This is how I like it, no cars and no people, just me, engulfed by nature. I sit in my car, enjoying a nip of malt and listen to Irish radio.

Tonight Pope John Paul II dies.

I awake to nature at its best, a vivid orange ball rising over the hills signalling the start of another new day. Sadly, my throbbing head brings me back down to earth with a bump. I decide that I will give drink a rest for a day or two.

I call Ruth and she tells me all about her forthcoming business trip to Australia. But this is a fast moving trip and unfortunately we have little time to talk. Already, waiting outside the Gigha shop, is Kenny, the man who will get me over to Cara. He is a solid built man but gentle with it. We arrange to meet at 11.00am on the south pier. It is a mad ten-minute rush to get my entire kit ready, but I make it.

Although Cara is my third uninhabited island, this will be the first time I have been on my own from being dropped off to being picked up. Across the water I can see Gigalum, a small island under 40 hectares, and further to the south Cara, my island number 30, which rises out of the ocean majestically, inviting me to come and visit her.

As Kenny appears in his boat, I am surprised to see how small it is. Similar in style to a rowing boat but made of fibreglass, its interior is painted a light blue colour with a dark blue exterior. The boat is meticulously maintained. Kenny explains that it is powered by a brand new outboard motor, which cost him £1,700 this season, having part exchanged his old one. The boat's oars sparkle so much, they look as though they have been polished. There is no doubt that this boat is Kenny's passion. I am fascinated to learn about its sonar equipment, which detects fish with great success, although catching them is another matter, he laughs. Working one week on and one week off on the Calmac Gigha ferry, it is plain to see that Kenny is at one on his boat in these waters, what a joy to see such a zest for life.

He tells me about the Brownie of Cara, who is the ghost of a MacDonald, murdered by a Campbell. As a result, no Campbell or relation of a Campbell can ever be taken to Cara. It seems that the Brownie lives in Cara House, which is the only house on the island.

Kenny drops me at the northern tip of the island. In front of me are ruins of an old bothy, an assortment of other abandoned buildings, and beyond these I can see Cara House, home of the Brownie.

In keeping with tradition, I raise my hat to the Brownie as I step ashore. I walk towards the house, the land looks good for camping and so I erect my tent right in front of it. Hopefully I'll be safe for the night.

I understand that the house is sometimes occupied by its owner, who is a friend of Kenny's. It has a very traditional 1950's look to it and I decide that I love it.

At each end is a black corrugated lean to and a chimney; it has two skylight windows, five windows on the upper floor at the front and four on the lower floor. All the windows are painted black, as are the double front doors. There standing in front of all this is my tent.

Today is the first fully uninhabited island that I have slept on, and also the first time that I have erected my tent on an uninhabited island. I must admit that I'm feeling rather nervous camping in front of this particular house, the home of the Brownie. I guess it's just mind games taking over, but being alone on an uninhabited island with a ghost.....

I set off to explore. Along the east shore, facing the Kintyre peninsula, the ground is fertile, relatively flat and green. Towards the south-east corner of the island, set upon a ledge is the Brownie's Chair. It is a huge slab of stone in the shape of a one armed armchair. It is just to the east of the highest point of the island, the Mull of Cara which is 56 metres. As I am walking towards the Brownie's Chair, I get my first glimpse of the feral goats. Reaching the Chair, I rest in it for a while, feeling at ease with my surroundings. I start to realise how much these islands bring out the essence of me.

From here, I continue my walk around the southern tip of the island, where I disturb a tiny kid; it can't be more than a couple of weeks old. It looks lost and nervous as it runs away, whilst turning its head to give me a final once over.

I pause to watch some gulls gliding in the wind. It must be amazing to be free like a bird; they are so at one with nature. From the rocks, cormorants look out to sea in search of their next meal. Here the waters seem reasonably calm, but I am aware of the power that lies therein.

As I head northwards along the west coast, the vegetation turns into solid heather. The centre of the island becomes a carpet of heather. In places I am struggling to walk through it. From this end of the island I can see Cara House sitting, isolated, in the distance. I find it quite hard to describe how I am feeling. I guess it's a mixture of being at one with myself combined with a sense of naivety. Is Cara a typical uninhabited Scottish island or is it quite unusual?

All along the north west coast are numerous tiny rocks and islets.

I make my way back to my tent for the night, unaware of what it is I am truly experiencing. I suppose it's like the first time you have sex, it was good compared with nothing, but how will it compare with the next night, the next partner, or the next island? Naivety and inexperience are wonderful things.

As I button down the hatches for the night, it all feels decidedly eerie. The night is very windy, wet and cold. I suppose my true experience of Cara will only be fully complete in the future, for we observe with our minds. Our minds are dependent on experience, mine in this field is limited.

It has been such a cold night and there has been heavy rain, although remarkably I have slept reasonably well. As I place my kit in my pack, I notice that the top has broken. Was it the Brownie?

I take a stroll around the house area, to the rear is a decomposed goat; nature is nature but it sure does stink. I make my way to the north of the island, where I am going to be picked up. The cold wind is biting my face. As I gaze seawards I marvel at its' blueness. Beyond I see the wind turbine on Gigha, and in the far distance the Paps of Jura. I wait for Kenny to arrive and shelter behind a wall to protect myself from the wind. Without the sharp wind, Cara is perfect.

After looking back towards the lonely isolated house, I turn to see Kenny starting to appear. He is wearing his orange waterproofs. At times, he is so low in the water that he almost disappears. As he struggles to find a place to pick me up safely, it suddenly hits home about the challenges I will face, on my trips ahead, with different tides and swell. I move across the bay to some different rocks and finally get onto the boat. Today it's a Force 6 with a Force 8 predicted later. Kenny's boat will only manage up to a Force 7. As we enter the open, unsheltered water, the sea turns decidedly lumpy.

Yet crossing at a slow pace is quite tranquil and as the boat glides across the water, its rhythm is soothing. In addition, keeping us company along the way, we are joined by flocks of Cormorants who choose to dive near to us, one narrowly missing my head as it slips off the boat into the sea.

Kenny has worked on the ferry for six years and, once he managed to get past the challenges of dealing with the public, he has settled into his one week on, one week off lifestyle. Arriving back at a different pier on Gigha, he drives me back to collect my car in his 4 x 4. A true gent.

As I head to the snack bar, buoyed by my experience of spending a night alone on Cara, I feel a real toughie. However afterwards, as I stand shivering in the relentless wind, enjoying a hot coffee and watching two small children eat their ice creams I start to question who is the toughest now?

After an abortive attempt to purchase a replacement pack in Oban, I head for Fort William, where I park up for the night, three miles out of town.

Opening my sleepy eyes, I am greeted by the sight of hailstones bouncing off my car. Last night I had parked in the dark, but this morning I am in awe of this most breathtaking of surroundings. All around me are green hills, with snow-covered mountains beyond. Although I am only a short distance from the activity and noise of Fort William, the few houses here awaken to the bleating of sheep. It is so peaceful.

It has been a hard couple of weeks. Yes, it has been an awesome time, but I am getting more exhausted, especially mentally. I phone Ruth and we decide that we will spend a night together on Saturday. She will drive seven hours up from Yorkshire. It will be good to touch base with her, as well as re-grouping my thoughts, my body, and myself before I go into the second stage of this trip.

So, a total change of plans! I buy my new pack then head to Oban to book our hotel for Saturday night. I decide to splurge out on a nice four-star hotel. After such a long journey for Ruth, it will be perfect.

Next, it's onto Kennacraig, ten miles south of Tayinloan on the Kintyre peninsula. I have travelled 300 miles just to buy a new pack and change my plans! I am still wondering about the Brownie, what a crazy time it has been! I start to look forward to Saturday and my spirits lift.

At Kennacraig terminal I clear out my kit and throw away my old pack. It is a great place to re-arrange things; this terminal is all shiny and new. From here, I phone my contact for Texa, he'll arrive back on Islay from Ireland tomorrow, we hope.

I like the people on the Islay ferry; they seem less tourist brigade than on the other ferries. As always the food on the Cal Mac ferry smells fantastic. I settle for a plate of chips, vegetables and salad washed down with some Irn Bru. I ask myself "Why do people put their feet on seats without taking their shoes off first? Don't they have any manners? Other folks have to sit on the seats after you've wiped your feet on them."

Everything is in darkness as I land, late at night, on Islay, island number 31. I turn right into Port Ellen, past the distilleries of Ardbeg, Laphroig and Lagavullin until I see that the road has come to an abrupt halt with a gate across it. I decide to call it a day and park up for the night, with the hope of better weather in the morning. Although, judging by the wind and rain tonight, it is not looking very promising.

The night is heavy, blustery rain. On the shore line in front of me, I keep seeing illuminated eyes, sheep's eyes. In the middle of nowhere, it is quite eerie.

The weather has been bloody freezing all this trip, never above 10 degrees celsius, add the wind chill, and I start to realise why my spirits have been low. I decide that I need some warmer, waterproofed gloves.

"There is no such thing as bad weather, just the wrong clothes." Have you ever been to the islands of Scotland?

The thought of going round another whisky distillery does not interest me, sacrilege I know. Instead, I treat myself to a 16-year Lagavullin miniature; it'll go down a treat tonight.

On the way back to Port Ellen, I stop off at Kildalton to take the obligatory photo of the cross. It is a much photographed scene but in the early morning light, although it has an austere look, its presence is serene and welcoming,

As I make my way northwards from Port Ellen to Bowmore I come across vast areas of peat, some of it has been cut and left out to dry, and some of it has been bagged up. It's the first time I have come across such a raw environment, which provides fuel. The roads across Islay are straight and wide and, in parts, almost like motorways. In fact, in some places, you feel that you're not on an island at all, particularly when you can't see the sea.

I pass the Round Church at Bowmore and then head towards Port Askaig for the ferry to Jura. In the Post Office at Port Askaig I'm surprised to read the funeral notices, which invite friends to attend. It is a very different way of doing things here. The road, which continues onto Port Askaig, is a new one. If I wanted to, I could free wheel all the way, downhill, along its hairpin bends.

At Port Askaig the ferry to Feolin, Jura, my island number 32, only takes five minutes. However, I have to be patient and wait, with another car, whilst a fuel tanker is ferried across first; fuel and passengers cannot be transported together.

Jura, with a population of 200 people and 6,000 deer, is a wild, rugged wilderness known best for the Paps and the Isle of Jura whisky distillery. Yet its true attraction is definitely in its harsh and dramatic landscape.

Apart for the occasional minor offshoot, the road on the island is a single track affair which goes from the ferry in the south, alongside the east of the island, to the island's northern reaches, where eventually you have to park up and proceed on foot. Jura itself is only about 30 miles in length, but it takes around one and a half hours to drive, such is the road condition with all its twists, dips and narrowness.

It is the most rugged island that I have seen so far. In some ways it is similar to Rum. For adventurous walkers and hill climbers Jura must be a dream. The Paps seem to be in a constant state of change from mist covered, to their magnificent best, when the wind succeeds in driving all the clouds swiftly past the island.

At Tarbet Bay, half way along Jura's eastern shores, a fertile grassy area appears where a dip in the road comes down to a bay. I am thrilled to see around 60 oystercatchers all feeding enthusiastically, in the safety of this little oasis. After some time, they take off together, a mass of orange beaks and piercing orange red eyes. Briefly, they fill the sky, but soon are gone, leaving me with the image of their eyes, which look like key holes to their souls.

At the end of the public road, a rugged car park is cut into the hillside. Further driving is made impossible by two rusted chains stretched across the road, padlocked onto two sturdy round posts.

A short walk along this path is Barnhill where George Orwell lived when he wrote the novel "1984." Beyond, at the island's most northerly tip, you can see the Gulf of Corrywreckan, the infamous whirlpool, which is overlooked by the island of Scarba, on the opposite side.

At this point, I walk back to my car, and, as I drive south, I am blessed with numerous sightings of deer, the most precious one, a stag with powerful antlers standing proudly amongst some small trees and rough grass. It has been an exhausting day. I park up for the night near to the ferry terminal and make plans for the morning.

My Lagavullin gets top marks. Tomorrow I will buy a full bottle!

Yet again, although it is exceedingly windy and bitterly cold I sleep brilliantly in the Skoda Hilton.

The ferry struggles to dock, its bow door is down. It almost docks, but then the current takes it back out to sea. After a large circle and a second approach, finally we have success.

I re-arrange the time for my ferry back to Kennacraig from Islay. Because of the bad weather, my contact is stuck in Ireland, so Texa will have to wait until next time. Today many ferries are cancelled, Armadale-Mallaig, the Small Isles, Orkney Ferries and Foula ferry all are. In bad weather, the Foula ferry is nearly always the first one to be abandoned, but today it seems that everyone else is affected too.

Undeterred, I decide to do a tourist circuit instead. Islay is an earthy island, it is not too touristy and for this, I love it, although I prefer the smaller islands, which I can fully explore, feel and be part of. The Gruinart RSPB reserve, to the north-west of the island, becomes my first port of call. Not just on the reserve, but all over, there seem to be geese, although I understand that most of them have already left for Greenland. It really must be wall-to-wall geese carpet when they are all here.

From here, after stopping in Bowmore, I visit The Oa, another RSPB reserve about six miles south of Port Ellen. Golden eagles can be seen here in the spring and the summer but today, with all this bad weather I don't catch sight of any.

I decide to park up above Port Ellen, with Texa in full view. The weather is certainly wild today, but Texa is still shining in the limited sun light. It is sad to see an island, almost touch it and know that you can't get to it; thoughts of Barra come flooding back. There are so many islands that I still need to to find a way onto. I pick up a bottle of Lagavullin whisky, a souvenir glass and put £10 worth of petrol in my tank. On Islay it is 10p a litre more expensive than on the mainland.

I visit the White Hart Hotel in Port Ellen and treat myself to a small beer and a whisky. The whisky menu looks quite inviting, shame about my wallet. Eventually I am onboard the 8.30pm ferry, although it doesn't actually leave Islay, because of the bad weather, for another hour and a half.

I am starting to see this adventure as a slow build up. Gradually, these islands are starting to unfold. I am being kitted out physically, but more importantly mentally at each stage. The mental side is vital and cannot be underestimated. After this last week of very cold weather and failed attempts, my mindset for visiting the 162 islands seems to be a kind of blind faith. Yes, I can call it off at any time, but it is such an adventure, and it makes me feel at one with myself.

Next week I will have to face eight islands, eight nights under canvas. I will have to rely completely on my mental and physical ability to handle all that nature might throw at me. Wow! It's O.K. I'm not losing my nerve, but I certainly don't know what to expect.

I'm starting to believe more and more that someone or something is looking down on me. When I look at the sea, I know what a monumental challenge this is going to be. But, I genuinely believe that I will achieve it and not die in the process. After all, to complete it is part of my journey. These islands will allow me to spend the night with them, when the time is right. Am I nervous? Yes, in a way I am. It's the unexpected, the not knowing what lies ahead and how to deal with it. So far I have spent one day in isolation, but eight plus?

At 2.00am, I park up ten miles south of Oban for the night.

I am up again at 7.30am and phone Ruth. Tomorrow we will meet at 10.00am for 24 hours of love. It seems so surreal, a bit like the Last Supper.

Next week starts the biggest challenge of my life, spending a night alone on each of these eight islands. If I had the ability, I would produce a best selling book to share my story, but I am aware of my failings with the written word. However, I believe we are all stepping-stones, and others will come forward who can give greater written justice to these islands than I. Although my education is almost non-existent, what I do possess is passion and this I can rely on.

In Oban I improve my kit, purchase a better fitting hat and some waterproof, thicker, warmer gloves.

Once more, it is time to board the Mull ferry. Having passed through Mull several times already, I have never actually spent a night there. Tonight, I shall do so. Mull will become my island number 33.

I book into a B&B at Craignure, which is within walking distance of the ferry. It is time to sort out my paperwork, have a shower, wash my hair, and look forward to the morning. After a couple of drinks in the local bar, it is time for bed.
Following a good night's sleep, I am on the first ferry back to Oban. Today is a day off.

Ruth arrives from Yorkshire for the day, having broken her overnight journey at Crianlarich. We are both really excited to see each other, rendezvousing for a "romantic" breakfast at Tesco's, after which we book into our lovely hotel on the Oban promenade.

Later, we pay a visit to Luing, my first island of this trip. It all seems surreal; Ruth being in Oban for the day, our looking together across the water towards the islands I am feeling nervous about. I wish I could say that our looking at them helped to calm me, but I can't. Some of them are covered in mist, others are just mere dots.

Later next week I will be out there.

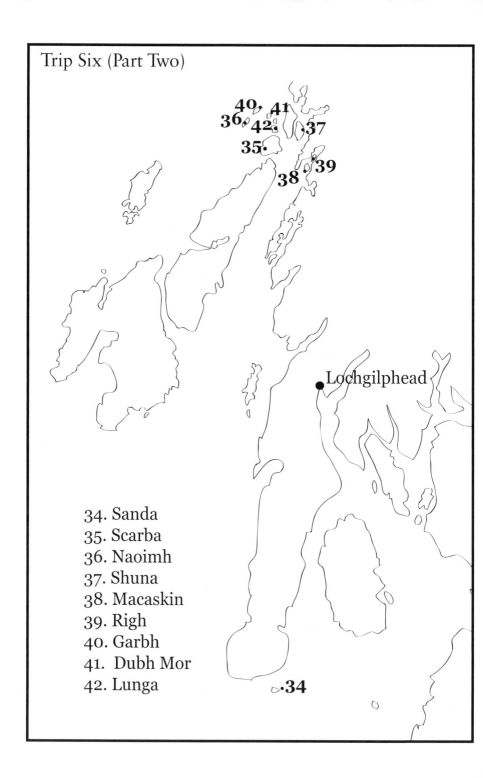

Trip Six (Part Two)

40, 41
36, 42, 37
35,
38, 39

Lochgilphead

34. Sanda
35. Scarba
36. Naoimh
37. Shuna
38. Macaskin
39. Righ
40. Garbh
41. Dubh Mor
42. Lunga

34

10

The Road Trip – Part Two

Sunday 10th April 2005
to Friday 22nd April 2005

Yesterday was romantic, sharing my world, my islands, with Ruth. It also helped Ruth come to terms with them. She said that the islands didn't seem too far away and, in a way, she was right. Yet what looks like only a short crossing can often be treacherous, if not impossible, given the wrong wind direction or too big a swell. If I manage to get onto all of these eight islands, in one attempt, it will be a major achievement. We still wait to hear from Righ, after numerous attempts to seek permission.

Our goodbye is hard, with tears in my eyes and a lump in my throat, I wave goodbye as Ruth drives out of Oban.

Ruth has left and the eight islands await, so let's be on with it! I drive to the supermarket, rearrange my car, do some shopping and head south to Campbeltown.

Last night we had a Mexican. I being of the male species ordered the food, which meant that we over ordered. However, the good news is that today I have lots of doggie bags!

I like Campbeltown, but it's a town, which appears frozen in time. The harbour is fantastic, possibly the best I've seen, yet there's no activity. Even the main hotel is closed for refurbishments. However, there are boy racers in abundance.

I decide to leave and visit the Mull of Kintyre instead. The drive to the top, where I park my car, is amazing. From here, I follow the steep path downhill for over a mile until I reach the lighthouse. It's a beautiful setting, with the sun glistening on the grey sea and far away, in the distance, I catch my first glimpses of Ireland.

To my left, I can see Sanda Island, which I am hoping to visit tomorrow. Beyond, in the distance, rising like a muffin out of the sea, is Ailsa Craig.

Meg, who is the wife of Dick, the owner of Sanda Island, has left me a message on my home answer machine. The boat may not go out in the morning, but she'll phone again tomorrow, before lunch, to let me know what's happening.

I park up on a quiet country road and bed down for the night.

I awaken to a beautiful spring morning with bright sunny skies. I'm optimistic that the Sanda boat will sail today.

Generally trying to pass time, I drive around, go to the toilet and buy a newspaper. After this, I give Ruth a call, knowing that we will be out of contact for a few days. Then I ring my answer machine, the boat leaves in fifteen minutes!

The Seren Las is filling up with diesel, I am her only passenger. She is the main supply vessel for the island, so today the boat is travelling at a loss. I realise how fortunate I am to be visiting such beautiful places, but for the people who live in these isolated locations economics is another story. The one hour, 13-mile, crossing to Sanda, my island number 34, is delightful. Directly ahead of me, in the distance, Ailsa Craig looms, I look forward to visiting her another day.

As we pull into Sanda's small pier, Dick Gannon, the island owner, is there to meet the boat. In the bay, there are three cottages, a bar cum restaurant and a farmhouse. All of these have either been renovated or built by Dick. Towards the rear is a library and games room. In the far corner of the field is a bunkhouse, this will be my home for the next two nights. After enjoying a fascinating conversation with Dick in the bar, it is time to settle into my new accommodation.

Dick is a small bearded man with the determination of an ox. He calls a spade a spade and clearly does not hold the local council, and all its red tape, in high esteem. I admire him, for he is definitely the sort of man who gets on with things and works his way around obstacles. What he has achieved on Sanda Island is inspirational.

His island bar, the Byron Darnton Tavern, has got to be one of the best hostelries in Scotland. Stocking over thirty whiskys, an extensive selection of fine wines and real ales, as well as wonderful food, this tavern is one of Sanda's gems. Such is its fame that apparently visitors from the mainland and from Ireland, regularly pop over to enjoy a night out. There is also talk of starting a darts team, but I reckon even the home team will struggle to turn up, and don't dare mention the winter league!

I take a walk southwards across the island towards the lighthouse. To my left is the neighbouring island of Glunimore, which is less than 40 hectares. As I reach the lighthouse, I am impressed. It is certainly the most unusual one that I have ever seen. Connected by a perimeter wall at ground level, are a series of old lighthouse keeper's cottages. But inside the wall, hewn into the actual cliffs upon which the lighthouse sits, are two modern cylindrical structures. Each cylinder is peatish brown in colour. The first cylinder, based at ground level, has a front door, which leads upwards to three further floors, each with their own small window. From the top floor of the first cyclinder, you walk through into the second cylinder. The second sits fractionally behind the first, again tucked neatly into the cliffs. This cylinder rises over another four floors, each with its own window until finally you are able to access the lighthouse. It is truly is amazing. If this is not enough, to the right directly adjacent to the lighthouse, is a natural arch. What a unique lighthouse setting.

After this interesting find, I head out along the island's east coast. This part is quite hilly with many sea birds on its cliffs. Occasionally I notice a dead sheep, which has failed to navigate the rocky crags. Sanda also has a lot of fertile, soft pasture, most of it suitable for grazing, some more rugged, but on the whole it is comfortable to walk on. Dick is looking after it well, with excellent, well maintained fences and gates.

I come full circle, reaching St. Ninian's Chapel and the old graveyard. It is an atmospheric place. A vast cross, although exceedingly weathered, dominates the graveyard. To the south of the graveyard, set in the shadow of the hills is a loch, surrounded by sheep. It is a beautiful scene.

After a turnaround at the bunkhouse, I head for the bar. I am not on my own for long. Soon I meet up with Dick, Rob who is a bird ringer, and Steve and Sue, a couple who are the island caretakers. Dick, a man who is never short of something to say, holds court. He has brought Sanda into the 21st century. These islands need a lot of people like Dick. Some may say he's outspoken, and they may be right, but this outspokenness is part of the character that has been needed to knock Sanda into shape. I find Dick's passion a joy to be around.

Steve and Sue arrived here last October and, having got through their first winter, now face their next big challenge, dealing with the public. Rob, the bird ringer seems completely at peace with himself. Currently, he is converting the old boat shed into a building for himself and the other bird ringers. Sanda is one of four island bird observatories around Scotland, along with North Ronaldsay, Fair Isle and the Isle of May.

After such an enjoyable evening, I enjoy an unbelievable nine hours sleep. This is unheard of for me. It must be the natural ventilation of the bunkhouse. Whatever the reason, I feel fully refreshed and so, straight after breakfast, I head off around the second half of the island, this time in an anti-clockwise direction. Having so much time to explore, Sanda is giving me the space I need to switch off and settle my mind, in preparation for the next eight islands.

The north-west side of the island is windy and exposed, with high cliffs. I sit overlooking the sea, listening to the electrifying symphony of birds, sea and the wind, each equally important in their own contribution to the magical sounds of Sanda. It is a perfect island, quite possibly my number one so far.

There are many reasons why I think this island should have such a lofty claim to number one, the accommodation, the soft ground, the pub, and the people here. In addition, walking around the island is so accessible with plenty of tracks available, albeit suitable for Dick's quad or just the sheep.

I reach the lighthouse once more. Approaching it from the east this time, it appears as though it is perched on the rock, which looks like a mini Ailsa Craig. From this angle, I can also see how difficult it must have been to have made the lighthouse accessible.

One day I would love to do a TV series on my favourite Scottish islands. I look forward to finding an island, which is more perfect than Sanda. I lie down in the long grass on the north coast and, assisted by a breeze and the relaxing sounds of nature, nod off into a comfortable sleep.

Awaking, feeling refreshed, I call in at the pub and end up chatting to Sue. I ask how she and Steve came to be on Sanda. Evidently, they saw it advertised under local jobs in their job centre…..in Devon!

It's quiet in the bar. One day I'd like to come back when it's busy, but, for tonight, I'm more than happy listening to Dick. His stories about the visitors to Sanda captivate and amaze me.

I am surprised just how disrespectful some people can be. I hear about the obnoxious attitude of some of the yachties. You would think that having the means to buy or charter a yacht, would bring out decorum and respect for others and for the environment, but sadly, this does not appear to be the case.

Bearing this in mind, I think it's really important for me to be fully transparent and wherever I can, to seek the owner's permission to visit their island. Already, having heard Dick's tales, I can fully understand why island owners and conservation groups are hesitant to allow people, not just to visit, but also to stay overnight on their islands.

I remember being told in the game parks of Africa..."Take only photographs, leave only footprints." - Too right.

The morning has a chill in the air, yet the sun is still managing to shine occasionally through the blue skies. Amazingly, I have slept for nine hours again. This bracing sea air obviously agrees with me.

The boat leaves at 12.00 noon, so I pack, sweep out the bunkhouse and put my pack in the entrance of the cottage nearest to the pier. Dick kindly invites me in for a cuppa. This man should write a book about his experiences on Sanda, he's such an interesting person to listen to. When I suggest this, he tells me that he's forgotten most of it. Well, he seems to remember a lot, what a great guy.

The boat arrives but no one is in any rush. I walk back to the bar, perch myself on one of the bar stools, and have a beer. The two boat lads, lifeboat men in their day jobs, call in for some soup and a beer. Rob and Dick join them.

Finally, we all bid our farewells. It is sad to say goodbye to such great people and such a special island. One day, I know I will return. What my island experience will be by then, I have no idea.

The boat back to town is rolling quite a bit, but it's nothing for these lifeboat lads. Just as well for me that my sea legs are slowly beginning to appear.

I give Ruth a quick call, do a shop in Campbeltown, then take the 50-mile journey northwards to Lochgilphead. Here, my first stop is the Chinese Takeaway, where I treat myself to a vegetable curry and chips, after which I pay a visit to Lochgilphead swimming pool for a shower, and the chance to wash and blow dry my hair. After this I make a few business calls and drive into Crinan to find out where everything is. Crinan has a twee feel to it, as well as a definite air of affluence.

Mentally I am feeling strong. I can see the boat, which will be taking me out tomorrow. As I walk across the road, to get a better look, I am aware that my chest is sticking out. This is going to be an amazing adventure, possibly the greatest of my life. Tomorrow I will progress from being a tourist, or a traveller, as every tourist likes to call themself nowadays. But, progress towards what? An adventurer? Am I becoming an adventurer? Me? Mr Non-Athletic? Wow!

The weather in Crinan is so mild that I could almost walk about in my tee shirt. I know my mind is ready for what lies ahead. My kit is ready and I am ready. Now it is time to park up and go to sleep. Tomorrow is the start of the biggest adventure of my life!

After a maximum of six hours sleep, the alarm goes off at 5.30am. Before a trip, an adventure, I never sleep that well. Maybe it's excitement or perhaps I am just plain nervous? I put my sleeping bag into my pack and eat some breakfast. This morning I have awoken to possibly one of the finest sunrises of my life, I hope that it will be a good omen.

I pick up two stones for my car wheels. As usual, I'm leaving it in gear with the handbrake off. This done, I make my final call to Ruth. If all goes to plan, we won't speak to each other for over a week. Its one of those, what can you say type of phone calls. We are both tense, but really, there's nothing left to say except, "Let's get this show on the road!"

I unload my kit from the car, a 65 litre backpack; a 25 litre day pack; a ten litre water bottle; jacket; walking stick; wellington boots and my number one mate, Clyde. It certainly looks a lot of kit against the car, but considering it's for eight days, it's not that much really.

The water is still, the early morning sun is beaming down and the boats are hardly moving. Hamish, the owner of Gemini, the boat I'm going out on, arrives. He has done a lot of groundwork for me, I really am grateful for the trouble he has taken. He is around my age, roundish in the face, with a liking for Regal Kingsize.

Hamish's boat is a catamaran. The last time I went out on one of these was on the Great Barrier Reef in Australia. Then, I almost drowned…..I hope not this time. We pass the time of day. I like Hamish, he seems a decent fellow, with a, hopefully, sound and expanding business, that he's just taken over.

As he drops me off onto Scarba, my island number 35, I notice two farm workers who are going further across the island. Hamish has OK'd my visit with the owners, so I have no need to worry. By the time I get off the boat, they have gone to work, around the other side of the island.

After one failed attempt, I manage to set up camp. I have managed to acquire my first bent tent peg in the process. I am camping close to the drop off point, so I don't have to carry my kit too far tomorrow. Scarba will be one of the few islands in the next eight days that has a pier. Once the tent is up and my kit set out, I am ready to start exploring.

Half way between my campsite and Kilmory Lodge, I come across a feeding area for the Highland cattle. It's really blathery. I walk through it; continuing past the Lodge and eventually coming to rest on a heather covered rock. The sun is shining, and as I sit here, I reflect on what an amazing life I have. Me, Andy Strangeway, son of a Wold's farm worker, who has spent most of his life in a council house, is here on an isolated Scottish island called Scarba, embarking upon the most amazing adventure of his life.

I can see Luing now, the island that Ruth and I visited only a few days ago, and to its right is Shuna. Lunga and the Fladda lighthouse are straight ahead. I love my maps. Sitting here with the sun in my eyes, they begin to come alive. How can it be possible for a man with such humble beginnings as myself, to have such an amazing dream come true? I could cry.

Scarba is hilly, it is the tenth highest of all the 162 islands. I look across at Lunga and wonder where I will set up my camp when I visit. Strange as it may seem, I know that these islands are just waiting for me to visit them. Why me, when no one else has ever done it before? I don't know. What I do know is that if I allow it, my thoughts will prevent me from visiting the islands, in the same way, that my thoughts will bring me to them. Now I do cry and then I laugh at the joy of it all.

I continue walking, watching some red deer jumping over fences in the distance. They become aware of me and stop their antics to stare. Scarba is a great island for deer because of the high terrain. Reaching a stream with a three feet gap, I wish that I was as agile as them. But I'm not, so I retrace my steps, run, jump and just make it. Well I have never said I was athletic!

I make my way to the southern part of the island from where I can see Jura, between which is the Gulf of Corryvreckan and the infamous Corryvreckan whirlpool with its speeds of over ten knots. It is one of the most difficult pieces of water in the world, to navigate.

After some very strenuous walking over heather, bogs and wet ground, I eventually reach Cruach Scarba. At 449 metres, it is the highest point on the island, and dominates the other islands that I shall be visiting in the next week. Walking across the top of the island, scattered with lochs, rivers and bogs, is extremely hard work. But, the slog is worth it, and my view is possibly the most breathtaking sight I have had from all of the islands so far. From here, I am able to see Jura, Islay, Colonsay, Mull, Easdale, Seil, Luing, Shuna, Dubh Mor, Garbh and Naoimh. It is just awesome.

I watch as a Calmac ferry goes by and realise that it's the Colonsay ferry. How my adventure has changed since Ruth and I visited Colonsay, even since my last Calmac journey, which was less than a week ago. Mind you, I could murder a plate of chips and a beer right now!

The walk back to camp is arduous; there seem to be bogs everywhere. The pounding on my legs today has been heavy; they are exhausted, right up to my hips. At the end of the day, I'm not some super fit machine, just a normal guy with a dream. As I look across at Dubh Mor, I must admit that I'm a little apprehensive about where I am going to set up camp. It looks very inhospitable to me.

I am so relieved to get back to my tent. Exhausted, I cook some Bombay potatoes and make a coffee.

I awake after half an hour, the coffee is stone cold. However, feeling less tired, I start to write up my journal. There's a strange noise outside. I open the tent door and peer round it. One of the Highland cows is staring straight back at me! I wave my stick at him, he moves on and I settle back down to writing my notes.

Is that the cow again? I grab my stick and peer outside once more. This time, to my consternation, about 40 Highland cattle are now within feet of my tent!

Oh shit! Do cows trample Yorkshiremen's tents? The answer is "quite possibly yes." I jump out of the tent, pulling on my boots in the process. Quickly, I start to walk down the road towards the pier. The cows follow. The workers have all left now and I am alone with a herd of Highland cattle playing follow my leader. I jump over the fence at the pier and wait. Humans are the ones who fetch their food, I suppose. I wait and so do they.

Plan B. I walk back up the hill past my tent and slowly they follow behind. To my right, off the main track, are some trees. I increase my pace, whilst they continue to amble along up the hill. Before they see me, I am off the main track and hidden behind the trees. I find it hard to suppress a squeal of delight as they continue walking past me up the hill. Yes!

Back at my tent, I pour a well deserved whisky and decide to call it a night.

It's a windy night outside, but my biggest problem is that I'm on a slope and consequently keep sliding down my bed. Finally, when I can stand it no more, I get up and put my day pack below my feet. Going to the toilet proves to be another challenge. I'm dying to go, but it's bloody freezing, and a battle of the bladder ensues. Eventually, my bladder wins, so wearing only my tee-shirt, knickers, hat and boots, it's a mad dash out and an even quicker one back! You wouldn't believe how long it takes to piss at 6.15am when your dangly bits are suffering from frostbite.

Hopefully today, subject to the weather forecast, we will be going to the outlying islands. I enjoy my breakfast of chopped tomatoes, a coffee and the last two bread rolls. Bread is something I'm going to miss, I love my bread. Also, not being able to shower, and wash my hair for so long is going to be an experience.

I take my first load of kit to the pier to wait for Hamish. This morning it's as cold as it was on Inchmarnock. It's at times like this that a young man recognises the true value of central heating, a duvet and a nice pair of breasts. Today's forecast promises a maximum of 11 degrees celsius, with a touch of frost tonight. I will definitely be wearing socks in my sleeping bag!

Finally, I take down my tent and Hamish comes into view, just as I am reaching the pier. He is not alone; today his parents have also come for the ride, to give him a hand. We are going to Naoimh, which will be my island number 36. At 56 hectares, it will be the smallest island that I've visited so far. Our route takes us between Scarba and Jura and through the infamous Corryvreckan, which fortunately today is calm.

In no time at all we are at Naoimh. The boat steadies whilst I jump onto the rocks. It's my most adventurous landing yet. Once I am on firm ground, my kit is thrown across, and Hamish and his family bid me farewell.

We came here today because Naoimh is one of the two most outlying islands. Of the two, it also offers the worst place to land. Because the weather is looking good, it made sense for me to land on the more difficult of the two today. I certainly feel isolated out here, but it's a great feeling! The island is well maintained by Historic Scotland. Once I have climbed over the rocks, I find the perfect place to set up my camp, lovely grass on top of soil; it's flat, with not a stone in sight.

As I sit in my new camp site, facing south, I can see the steep cliffs of Scarba's west coast. Even from here, it looks a hard island, definitely the big brother of the ones I am due to visit this week. Today, I am camping within 150 metres of my landing place, and rather than carry the full ten litres, I have left my water container close to the landing, in readiness for tomorrow's pick up. I'll make do with a small water bottle, which is in my pack, as I don't believe in exerting myself unnecessarily.

Evidently, a monastery was established on Naoimh 21 years before the one on Iona, yet, because of its inaccessibility, hardly anyone ever gets to see it. Seemingly, there is talk of ghosts being here, but I don't mind if I have a little company.

Naoimh is about one and a quarter miles long and a quarter of a mile wide. It's only a small island, and even before I start to explore it, I know that I am going to love it. It looks like it will be an easy island to explore and, after Scarba, I think I deserve it. On Scarba, I saw so few birds, yet already today, I've seen loads, including a flock of geese flying overhead. It is a real joy to be on one of the most isolated islands. I love this feeling of isolation.

The sun is much stronger than it was yesterday and now, after an initial cold start, it is getting warmer. Above all, it is idyllically peaceful here. After my camp is set up, it is time to explore. I haven't walked very far before I decide to stop and rest. This island has such an air of tranquillity; it makes me feel the same. Ahead of me is Jura, its Pap's shining in the sun, and beyond is Islay. Here on Naoimh, not far ahead, is a small loch, with two geese swimming on it. I watch them for a while. Eventually, they decide to take off, accelerating like planes on a runway, until finally they are airborne and floating effortlessly in the wind. I really ought to start moving. As I do, I notice on my right, a cliff, covered in meadow primroses, and in the distance Naoimh's small lighthouse.

The southern tip of the island is definitely gull territory; their calls resound in my ears. Not quite on the southernmost tip, is the lighthouse. It is a modern affair, none of your high round structures. This one is small and square, with iron rails around it. It looks more space ship than Scottish island, but hey, even on these islands, I guess technology moves on.

On that subject, Hamish has shown me how to contact the Coastguard on channel 16. "In case I break a leg or something," he says! Thanks! Joking apart, he thought it was best to leave his VHS transmitter / receiver with me. I guess it's almost a mobile phone, something which I don't possess.

Along the south-west coast are steep cliffs, their rock is a hard, sharp substance, which has a moon like appearance. Like most of these islands, the beauty appears in the harshness of the landscape, although this is something of a contradiction, for Naoimh in so many ways, is a soft gentle island, albeit in an isolated location.

I walk northwards along the top ridge of the island's western side. Directly below me is a sheer drop, but eastwards the decline to the sea is much gentler. At the 80-metre O.S. marker, I secure Clyde in my walking stick handle for his photograph. This is to prevent the wind from whisking him out to sea. It's very strong up here, which initially results in both Clyde and the stick being blown over. Fortunately, they are both O.K. so I re-position them and the second attempt is successful.

From this high point, I head back down to the campsite for some food. This sea air is powerful and once again, I fall asleep and wake up to a cold coffee. Today the weather has been the best of my trip, deep blue skies, fluffy white clouds and shimmering rich blue seas.

The time has finally come, I have reached the "Is this a beard or shall I have a shave?" stage. However, six days without a shave means that it won't be easy; also, I am going to have to find a water supply, which isn't saline. My personal freshwater supply is far too precious for me to use. Eventually I find a small questionable loch, and unbelievably manage to achieve a clean shave without any "nicks". As I am shaving away, thoughts of Crocodile Dundee keep coming into my mind. I wonder when was the last time anyone else shaved on Naoimh?

Feeling totally invigorated by this experience, I take a walk over to the semi-detached beehive cells. It is a lovely walk, made even nicer by my route being decked with glorious golden buttercups. O.K so maybe sometimes I do get the names of flowers and birds wrong, I do my best with only a limited knowledge. But hey, if I'm wrong, then I don't care. My desire is to experience, not to become an expert in anything other than my experience of these islands.

The north end of the island is much more rugged, with heather and briars on its lower ground. The high rocky ridge along the west coast runs its full length, from north to south. I sit at this most northerly extremity and admire a natural arch. It is beautiful, as all natural arches are, but it is not exceptional.

As I walk back to my tent I contemplate the people that people lived here over 1500 years ago. Most of the 162 islands have been inhabited at some time. They had a lot less equipment than we have, no waterproof jackets, cooking kits or radios. Yet they survived and prospered on these islands, whereby nowadays to stay one night is an achievement. We have all become soft.

If you believe all the stories, then Naoimh has many ghosts, but so do most of these islands. Why are we threatened by such stories, even if they are real? It's just a fear of the unknown. I spend my evening drinking a little whisky, enjoying the sounds of the islands and reflecting how fortunate I am not to be frightened by such things.

I awaken for two glorious hours at 1am. Getting up to go to the toilet, the night is cold, but the stars are shining and the moon is a bright crescent quarter. I return to the warmth of my sleeping bag, where I lie awake listening to the wind, the occasional sheep and the ever present gulls. Sleeping here in a place "full of ghosts," I am completely at peace. How could anyone ever imagine that it is a dangerous place to sleep? I don't understand it; a city, now that is dangerous.

When I re-awaken, it is raining heavily. I take down my tent and in only two journeys, I have transported my kit to the pick up point where I wait for Hamish. Jumping off rocks in dry conditions is relatively straightforward, but this morning it is wet and slippery, much more likely to be problematic.

Just as I get the last load of kit into place, Hamish arrives. As his boat draws in, the water carrier, which I left on the rocks yesterday, slips into the sea. It is hooked out of the water, having floated well, but the rescue has resulted in two holes appearing in it. It should be OK for today, but tomorrow Hamish will have to fetch the other ten-litre carrier from my car.

At 6.00 am, Scarba had disappeared into the mist. Now, all the mist has gone and I can see over to the distant mountains, which are covered in snow. According to my radio, back home in Yorkshire they've had snow too, with many roads blocked this morning.

It's good to see Hamish. Once again, he takes us through the Corryvreckan, but all is calm. The weather is forecast to blow up a bit over the next few days, so

Hamish will bring me back out to Garbh later, when things have settled down. In the meantime, I need to be more sheltered and less exposed to the elements.

As we cross the open waters, I look over to Scarba, now covered in snow down to 200 metres, the other day I was on her summit.

Landing on the north-west coast of Shuna, my island number 37, is a lot easier to get onto than Naoimh. However, Hamish only manages to steady the boat for a few seconds, just long enough for me to jump. Shuna is more sheltered and the rocks that I am jumping onto less rugged.

A family live on Shuna, so I'll not be sleeping solo tonight, but I'm well enough away from them in my isolated location so as not to be disturbed. I set up camp. Everything is a little damp from Naoimh.

Near to my campsite, is an abandoned lime kiln. Shuna has reasonable tree and shrub cover, which in its day would have been used as fuel for the kiln. I begin my walk across the island. My sense of direction being what it is, I end up going completely the wrong way! Eventually, after a battle with the vegetation, I manage to get myself back on the right track. One of the distinct advantages of visiting small islands is that you can't get lost for too long, even on Foula!

Near to Shuna House, on the north-east, is the island's jetty. Here, an old abandoned canoe rusts away alongside fish farms boats, anchored with their outboard motors in front of a larger boat. Also secured to this jetty, looking completely out of place, are a large number of sea worthy canoes. The whole area has an abandoned, past its sell by date feel to it.

The walk from Shuna House to Shuna Cottage on the south-west of the island is across a mile and a half of farm track. Even by Yorkshire Wolds standards, this path is, to say the least, "blathery." I have made a big mistake by not wearing my Wellingtons. My boots seem to be holding up reasonably well, but I am having to walk very deliberately and choose my path carefully. The mud at the shallowest point is over six inches deep, totally submerging my boots. Thankfully, it doesn't go over the tops.

After navigating the route across, I arrive at Shuna Cottage, where there are two abandoned buildings, one of which is similar to the kiln near my tent. There are pheasants here in abundance. The bay, which looks onto Shuna Sound, is perfectly still. It's so quiet that I realise my ears are still buzzing from the Status Quo concert I went to four years ago. Great concert though! I was on the front row and shook hands with Francis Rossi, the God of my youth. I could tell that he was jealous of my full head of hair!

I much prefer this side of the island with Luing across the Sound and Scarba beyond. I find the more sheltered east coast, which faces onto the mainland, less interesting.

I rest for a while, stopping to eat a few oatcakes and enjoy a drink of water, before I make my way back across the island. On the return journey, my walking stick sinks more than a foot into the waterlogged ground; my waterproof trousers are caked in mud.

Shuna House, a mock castle with pebble dashing, looks so kitsch. It reminds me of Vera Duckworth's house on Coronation Street. I come across the residents of the island, who seem a little hesitant. I suppose they don't get many people camping on Shuna. I certainly wouldn't recommend it. I explain to them where I'm camping and that Gemini has dropped me off, the owner having given me permission to be here.

Shuna has four holiday cottages. I hope that the road is more walkable when people rent one of them. The island has a sad, unkempt look to it, but possibly it's because of the amount of rain we've had.

I am glad to get back to my tent. After I've had some food, I decide to write a note to Ruth, which will be posted in the morning, compliments of Gemini's postal service! This tent has a real dampness to it tonight. But, as it was taken down in the rain, the ground is wet and I have seen no sun today, so what else can I expect? I feel that I've settled well into my island journey. Remembering how I felt only a few days ago, now I am relaxed and not at all nervous.

Tonight I am also feeling cold and damp. I'm glad of the whisky, which of course, is purely medicinal.

My alarm goes off. It is 5am. There is a brass band having one hell of a practice in my head. I didn't drink that much last night, did I? I hope they realise they will not be paid and push off home, preferably quietly, taking their noisy instruments with them. I fall back to sleep.

It's now 7.00am and I am in a mad rush. Hamish is due in one hour's time.

When I began this trip, I slept in a tee shirt and pants. Then my top got added;

now my socks and jeans have also joined the party. The advantage of this, as well as not turning into a block of ice quite so quickly, is that on mornings like this I am already dressed. I do reckon I must be starting to smell, but the sheep don't seem to mind and Hamish and his father are too polite to mention it.

There's a strong wind today and it takes three attempts to get the boat near enough to the rocks for me to throw my kit across. Just as we get it all onboard, and I am ready to go, the boat is gusted out again and I am marooned. Struggling to hold the boat, Hamish gives it all he's got, at which point I leap onboard and we are off.

On board, I empty the remains of the Yorkshire water from my injured water carrier and leave it with Hamish to dispose of, its replacement already waiting for me. I don't even attempt to roll up my tent. In these conditions, I just push it into a plastic bag. I am most grateful for the mug of piping hot black coffee which Hamish's father offers me. My poor head! The sea certainly is not helping matters; it is decidedly lumpy and set to get worse later today.

Hamish has only just taken over his business and has never landed people on some of these islands. So, for him too, it's a steep learning curve. We arrive at Macaskin, island number 38. It is relatively sheltered, but because of the wind, we can't get in. The sea is too rough and the swell too high.

So it's Plan B. Hamish phones a mate on a nearby fish farm, gets a number for the person working today and we are in business. Alex, at the salmon farm between Righ and the mainland, comes over in a "paratrooper type of landing vessel." It's a metal boat, the type used on these fish farms, a real work horse and great for landing onto rocks and beaches. All I have to do is jump from one boat onto the other and we're away.

Alex hasn't landed here before either. But where there's a will there's a way. To the north-west of the island, we find a suitable place for landing. After getting my kit onto the island, I push his boat away and wave him "thanks and goodbye".

Now to find a campsite. I have cliffs in front of me and the wind is picking up. I start walking south but realise that it's too exposed. I retrace my steps and make my way around the north end of the island, where I find a campsite to the east of the cliffs. Here, the wind drops noticeably. I spot some old wooden sheep pens with flattish, soft green grass; the ground doesn't seem too wet. This should be the best place to weather the storm.

Quickly I erect my tent, and bring in all my kit, this time including the new water carrier. The gods are with me, for just as I start to settle down inside, the drizzle turns to heavy rain.

The wind and rain is increasing, it is the most violent shaking my tent has had so far. My kit is on the right, but with the force of the wind, my inner tent wall is touching the outer. Quickly I transfer my kit to the left and start to mop up the damp with my little sponge. I have everything here that I need, waterproof boots, jacket and trousers, water, wellies, food, VHS radio, a book, a pen, cooking equipment, a warm sleeping bag, and last but not least, Clyde and my bottle of whisky. I devise a place between the outer and inner layers of my tent to hang up my trousers and jacket. This is a real success as it means that the inside of my tent will remain dry. All I can do now is hole up and let the storm pass.

I hear a helicopter overhead and wonder if it is from Righ. An approach will be made again today with a view to my staying overnight.

It's 2.00pm, and the BBC weather forecaster advises "severe gales in the south-west of Scotland." Is that right?

I wonder when I will be able to go walkabout? I've not left my tent yet, and already it's late afternoon. "Is my weight stopping this tent from taking off? Quite likely, yes."

As I listen to the storm attacking it, I can quite truthfully say I wouldn't change my current situation for anything in the world. I know that this will seem strange to many of you, but honestly, I am at peace here. I have no idea when this weather will pass, or how long I am going to remain on this island, but here in my tent, I feel as comfortable and safe as a foetus in the womb.

Shit, this wind is getting serious. The tent is shaking more violently than ever. It's turned 4.00pm and now it's looking like I am going to have to stay put until morning.

The wind roars as it hits the trees on the cliff above me. Seconds later, my tent starts to shake again, as the wind powers down the cliff and pounds into its canvas. This noise is deafening and my tent is shaking continuously. Is it going to hold?

The assault is unrelenting. The wind is now accompanied by torrential rain, sheets and sheets of it. The ground is becoming soaked and my tent floor is getting damp. It is now 7.00pm and I need to work out how best to keep everything as dry as possible tonight.

I am aware of the wind decreasing, although the rain seems to be getting worse. I must be sitting in the eye of the storm. If I were out in the Garvellachs, Naoimh or Garbh I would have had serious problems in these conditions. Hamish has played a blinder; here I am not too exposed to the wind.

Everything is relative.

It is now 9am on the 18th April, a new day and the storm has passed. I don't know what is planned for today; Hamish said that the pick-up would be later. I am fortunate, my tent hasn't flooded. O.K. it's damp from the wet rising up out of the ground, but that's not too much of a problem. I am 95% dry, and it certainly could have been a whole lot worse.

At daybreak, with the storm gone, I leave my tent and start to walk around the island. Along Macaskin's backside, the west coast of the island, is a high ridge. This is where the wind came roaring down yesterday. Of course, with all the rain, the island is sodden, not as bad as Shuna, mind you. Today Shuna must be horrendous.

Even where there is pasture on Macaskin, the grassy humps have rock underneath. East of the ridge are a couple of abandoned stone dwellings, which sit decaying back into the island. One has no roof or windows. The windows on the other one still stand firm, although its roof is half caved in. There is a reasonable amount of tree cover here. On a summer's day, Macaskin would be a delight to visit, but in the dampness of this early morning, after yesterday's violent storm, it feels a harsh environment.

There is a house standing at the southern tip of the island and a second, surrounded by woodland, on the north-east coast. Near the second house is a square wooden outside toilet. This house, which has a tin roof, has green wooden windows and doors. The curtains at the windows remain closed, although a water barrel has been carefully positioned to catch fresh water from the drainpipe outside. At the front of the house, which looks across to the mainland, is more rocky ground, covered in grass, and to its rear is woodland. A welcoming seat on the balcony, shares room with some fish trays and an old rope, which is hanging from the wall. In front of the wooden door, I notice an old saw bench. It reminds me of the type my father and I used when I was a child.

As I approach the house, I can see a lamb is dying on the ground. Sadly, there is nothing I can do for it.

Whilst I am out of the tent, I go to the toilet. Amazingly, yesterday during the storm I never needed to go, which was extremely fortunate.

Back at the tent, I wait. I am a little cold, so I get back into my sleeping bag. The sea looks calm enough in the sheltered water, but in the open waters, it can be quite a different matter. However, the forecast seems to be improving as the week goes on. Now, thankfully, the wind has left me and there are occasional light showers promised. Outside, the birds are singing, yesterday they were silent. Already today, I have seen a fishing boat and heard an aeroplane overhead; life is quickly getting back to normal.

I am certain that I must be starting to smell. Today will be my fifth day without a shower.

By 12.30, it is starting to look as if I will be here for another day, even though the sea appears calm. I start to acclimatise myself to the idea. It will be my first day, cut off, marooned so to speak. I stay in my sleeping bag to keep warm, and switch off the VHS to save the battery. I find lying back, contemplating is great. The next thing I know, it is 4.00pm, and I realise that I have been asleep! I awake and hear the sound of a boat. Quickly, I switch on the VHS and within seconds, Hamish's voice comes through.

He identifies my position and it's time to rock'n'roll! Let's move camp! The wind may have gone, but once again, the rain is torrential, the worst conditions I've had to move camp in, so far. But, hey, I love it! My tent is soaking. All I can do is take it down and screw it up. Within 20 minutes, we are on our way; it's only a few metres between Macaskin and Righ, my island number 39.

Hamish's wife is with him today. He introduces me to her as "the crazy man." I don't think I will bother trade marking it, but how about "Island Man," now there's a thought. After a hot black coffee and some great banter, it is time for me to jump onto the rocks of Righ.

In a matter of minutes, I have found somewhere to camp. I have left my boots on Hamish's boat, to dry, they're not excessively wet, but will benefit from a good airing. I won't need them, wellies definitely being the order of the day.

I realise that I have pitched the entrance to my tent within two feet of a 30-foot drop. If I fall, I will land on hard rock. I suppose it could be worse, with my swimming inabilities, it could have been into the sea. Regardless of my developing nerves of steel, the tent has got to be moved.

My new campsite is covered in briars. I remove as much of them as possible, hoping that the remainder won't rip my tent. Once it is re-erected, I head back to the landing place to fetch the rest of my kit. This is not as straightforward as it seems, as my route is now down a ten feet rock face. No worries! I start to lower myself gently; my right hand clamped firmly onto a two-foot square piece of rock. As I am peering below, looking for my next foothold, I feel the rock start to give and then, shit, down I go! It all happens so quickly, resulting in my making an undignified landing onto some soft grass, and the culprit rock narrowly missing me. Laughing out loud, I pick myself up and wander over to the landing to start moving my kit.

Two loads and finally everything is at base camp. Now it is time to re-group and dry out. My tent is like a Chinese laundry and there's a musty, damp smell inside. But, moving camps and islands in such conditions, what can I expect?

Some of my personal papers are a little damp too. I put them in my sleeping bag and then lie down on top. As I do, I take a look round my tent, and laugh. What a brilliant solo adventure this is. I have 123 islands left and I am ready for each one. I have no fear. In addition, I'm starting to meet some fantastic people, which is a part of the journey that I love.

In my tent entrance area, there are slugs everywhere. The bastards. I have spiders inside my tent and now a fly has moved in too. What is this, a nature reserve? I might as well just go for it, and invite all of the neighbouring sheep and their lambs to my party. What the hell!

I feel like a paratrooper, dropped in behind enemy lines. Although approaches have been made for permission to land, there has been no response. So, I have been dropped off at the end of the island.

The weather, from now until Wednesday, is forecasting some daily improvement. Tomorrow the sun is due to shine; it sounds so good. Thanks to Hamish's tactics, my plans have not been delayed. Only Texa has been postponed from the islands lined up for this trip, and with the weather improving day by day, I only have three left now with Hamish. This trip is turning out to be a real success. I certainly didn't expect to get onto Righ, that is a real bonus.

I don't think that there's anyone else on the island, but really, I'm not sure. In the morning, when I go walkabout around 6.00am, I will be discreet, but at the end of the day, you can only go so far when seeking permission to land. I believe I should respect island owner's rights and wishes, yet the Scottish Outdoor Access Code states that I can camp almost anywhere. However, for me, what is legal is second to what is morally correct.

The VHS is due to go on at 8.00am and by 9.00am, I should be gone. Hamish has promised to bring additional food supplies from my car, he has been a star. There is still a little rain, but I think the end of the storm is passing. I can even see where the sun is setting, just a bit of brightness glowing on the horizon through the clouds. The birds are singing and the mist is lifting.

As I enjoy a wee nip, I look forward to my walkabout in the morning and to my next three islands. All this bad weather has got me thinking. Wellies are a great invention for walking through wet conditions, but how do you stop rain coming in at the top? I suppose that waterproof trousers over the wellies are the answer. I really do need to get out more!

Fortunately, the weather is improving.

As the 5.00am alarm goes off, I realise that finally it has stopped raining. I am out of my tent, in less than half an hour, and ready to explore Righ. Being so near to Macaskin, Righ is quite similar, but without the ridge along its backside. I walk half way along the length of the island until a new agricultural type of building comes into view. The owner of the island is an unknown person, although there seem to be many rumours locally. Evidently, he owns two helicopters and a seaplane. I can make out the helicopter landing area from where I am standing. I don't think there's anyone else on the island, but really, I don't need the hassle if there is. As the clouds start to disappear and the sun comes shining through, I take a picture of Clyde on the highest point of the island, Dun Righ at 55 metres, and then head back to my tent to pack.

The day is opening up beautifully and the sea is looking unbelievably calm after the storm of the last two days. Beyond the mainland, the last few clouds are still hanging defiantly to the top of Scarba. I make two trips with my kit back to the pick-up point. I will be glad to leave, I feel uncomfortable on this island.

At the landing point, I work out a suitable place for the boat to come in, about six feet above the water level. However, because of the strong winds, it takes three attempts for Hamish to get close. My bags are passed quickly across, but just before the last piece of kit is onboard, the wind sweeps Gemini out again. Undaunted, Hamish holds her firm and powers back in again. My final bag is passed over, I jump the boat's rail and then at last, thankfully, we say goodbye to Righ.

Onboard, another warm black coffee awaits me. I restock my food supply with Hamish's delivery, from my car, and before I know it, Garbh is in sight. It has an old abandoned pier, which will make landing easier for me. As we pull into the bay on the south-east of the island, I take a two-foot leap and I am on dry land. After another "goodbye, Hamish, see you tomorrow," once again I am left alone, this time on Garbh, island number 40.

I walk along the broken down pier, past piles of wooden pallets, no doubt used as makeshift fences to herd sheep off the island. At the top of the bay, I can see a cottage. It's in reasonable condition, used as a bothy for the shepherd when he visits occasionally. In front of it, I'm thrilled to see a patch of perfectly maintained grass. Unable to resist, I begin to set up my camp there immediately. The cottage is well preserved, with its five windows and two doors intact. One of the doors has a porch and the other a step. The latter will make a very useful seat.

Camp erected, I settle my stomach with some food, and then sit on the step looking out to sea. From here, the sun is quite dazzling as it bounces off the water. After two days of storms, it is wonderful to see it again and to feel its warm rays. I hang my bags out on the nearby bushes to dry.

The sun feels good; it seems such a shame to move. So, why should I? Not needing any encouragement, I decide that today, I am going to laze about and enjoy the beautiful weather, glorious isolation and my perfect surroundings. I drag my mattress from out of the tent. It's sunbathing time! Fantastic! Here I am on Garbh, sunbathing in my wellies!

Not for long. Off they come, followed by my socks. Well, it is 13 decrees celsius here, an absolute heat wave! I am completely in holiday mood, and all caution is thrown to the wind. Off come my tee shirt and then my trousers. Wonderful! The occasional breeze is lovely, really quite cooling. I lie there, relaxing for a while. "Go on, no one will see you!" Slowly the small voice of temptation begins to become more insistent, until finally, it gets the better of me and, with a flourish, off come my kegs. Let it all hang out!

So, you get the picture. Here I am on an uninhabited island in Scotland in the middle of April. It's 13 degrees and I am sunbathing, stark bollock naked, with my wellies at the side of my sun lounger. How many people can ever say they've done that?

Class!

The afternoon is wonderful. I lie, here in this state of undress, for two hours; I feel no urgency to get up and explore the island.

Did I ever tell you about the man who decided to join the Scottish Naturists? He went onto their website to sign up. When he clicked onto the home page, it simply said, "Moved to Australia!"

Before I left Righ, I brushed my teeth, for the first time in five days and brushed my hair, the first in two days. Here, on Garbh, there is a delightful stream to the side of the cottage; buttercups cover the grass in abundance. Now a man in such situations starts to think. "That stream, why not? It can't be that cold." Not needing much persuasion, I decide to go for it, completely bollock naked. My first shower in six days. It is absolutely fantastic!

Soaking wet, I drip all the way back to my sun lounger to dry off. Once I am dry, I give my teeth a floss in the stream; the Denplan hygienist would be proud of me.

It has been so relaxing, resting here in the bay, drying my things out and cleaning myself. Oh yes, I nearly forgot the big event. Clean underpants; the first since Oban! No, I'm not going to work out how long ago that was. But, suffice to say, Clyde seems very happy at the new improved me. Before I put on my clean clothes, I decide that I need some evidence to show Ruth. So, using the reflection from the cottage's dirty window, I take a photo of myself with all my clean dangly bits blowing in the wind!

It's now 3.00pm. The birds are singing loudly, the sea is breaking onto the rocks in the bay and the sun is shining high in a perfectly blue sky. It is time to finish my coffee, wash the sheep shit off my bare feet, put on my socks and wellies and go walkabout.

I am disappointed to find a previous visitor has left the remains of his camp fire for all to see. I disagree with the need for open fires. After all this is private land. But, if you are going to have one, please be decent enough to tidy up after yourself. I think respect for an island is so important.

As I continue to walk around the island, I'm amazed to see about 50 deer. I wonder if they all swam across here from Scarba? Away from the bay, Garbh is rough and hilly. But finally, I reach its highest point, at 110 metres, and, as I enjoy some magnificent views from the top, I begin to realise that I'm on my way home. Dubh Mor and Lunga, my next two islands, lie across the water, between here and Crinan. I have been away for a month, visited over 20 islands; it has been the making of me.

Back at the campsite, I sit on the cottage doorstep, thinking of home and what it will be like to say goodbye to these islands. To my left is a magnificent rock face. It would look awesome on a housing estate in the middle of suburbia! As soon as this thought enters my head, a reply comes back in a flash, "It wouldn't last two minutes; it would be covered in graffiti in no time."

The colours, sounds and textures that have formed my life for the past month, will soon become special memories. When you see a few islands in the same group, you recognise that they have similar features. Whilst this is true, I also acknowledge that each island has individual and unique characteristics. Tonight I feel quite sad. These islands have become my world, yet soon the time will come to leave them, to re-adjust to what is "normal." I have a little malt and think about tomorrow.

As I get into my tent, I struggle with the zipper on the outside. Shit! It has broken. Eventually, I manage to work out a new system; the top zipper is still working, but the bottom one has had it. With only two more islands to go, I hope the top one lasts.

I come to, with the alarm ringing in my ear. I snooze for an hour, contemplate for another half an hour and then finally crawl out of my sleeping bag. It is 7.00am. The air on these islands is more powerful than any potion. I have progressed from preferring a hotel to my car, but now, sheltered in total isolation, amongst these spectacular islands, there is no place I would rather sleep than in my tent.

My breakfast of peanut butter and oatcakes again proves to be something of a challenge. Next time I will have to get the smooth variety, the crunchy one just breaks up the oatcakes. Sadly, I take down my tent. Garbh has been a haven for me, the place in which I said goodbye to a storm and hello to sunshine, blue skies and naturism. After two trips to the pick up point, Hamish appears. As always, he is on time. I switch off Terry Wogan, and prepare to jump on board.

It's a relatively straightforward boarding, Hamish and I are getting better at it. As I sit enjoying my coffee, he hands me a newspaper cutting with details of another charter company, situated in a different part of Scotland. It is information for another adventure, and one to be filed in my future contacts file.

Dubh Mor, island number 41, is bleak. Quintessentially it is rock. Looking at it, I wonder if we are going to be able to land there and where I will put my tent, if we do. However, Hamish is not intimidated by it; skilfully he manoeuvres Gemini in and out of the rocks. Three times, he tries, and on each occasion, he is unable to get close enough, due to the hidden rocks underwater. Then, finally, he's in! It's an extremely rocky drop off, and I'm forced to clamber over more rocks in search of anything that resembles a sheep path.

We have landed in an area just below the bay, to the north-east of the island. On my left, at 53 metres, is Dubh Mor's highest point, and on my right, Dun a Ghaill, a smaller hill. In the middle, a thin strip of land connects these two landmarks; it only rises a few feet above sea level. On either side, there is a pebble beach, with rough grass and heather flourishing in the middle. As the wind is coming in from the north, I make up my mind to set up camp on the southern part of the strip. It offers only a few metres of shelter, but every centimetre will help.

I am more than relieved, although somewhat surprised, when each tent peg sinks straight into the ground. Having worked out a makeshift system with the tent's broken zip; I install all my kit inside, blow up the mattress, get out my sleeping bag and then crash.

As I drift off to sleep, I can hear the gulls calling out overhead, what a fantastic sound.

I awake, a couple of hours later, to a sheep bleating outside my tent. Peering out, I am impressed by the cleanliness of his coat, although it's hardly surprising when I remember the recent weather. My new neighbour stares, and then runs off to tell his mates.

I'm so comfortable inside this sleeping bag. Many would say that I am wasting my time, arriving on an uninhabited island, erecting my tent, and then just going to sleep. But, at this point I do have the time, the time to lie down and allow the island to envelop me. To me, it's not about seeing this and that, it's also about feeling an island.

There is no record of anyone ever having lived on Dubh Mor, the only such island amongst the eight. There are two main reasons for this, accessibility and water. Dubh Mor is very difficult to get on and off, secondly, it has no water supply. Having said all that, I love it! I feel that, the more a place is exposed to human contact, the more it becomes affected by it. I guess you would say that its energy has changed. Dubh Mor, has a pure energy, it is unadulterated by human beings. Many would claim Iona has a special energy, but what are they comparing it to, Mull, Oban, Glasgow or even London? Most people will never experience the energy that is on an island like this. Sadly, for so many, Iona will be the best that they will ever encounter. Before I even leave my tent, I know that I will love Dubh Mor.

After some lunch and coffee, it is time to go walkabout.

I climb to the top of Dun a Ghaill, at 35 metres it is the second highest point on the island. I sit there, soaking in the serenity of my surroundings. Straight ahead of me is the island's highest point. Below it, the raised beach looks like a pile of pebbles. Between these two points is the thin strip of land where I have put my tent. Up here, it looks small and exposed.

Behind me is Fladda lighthouse, the biggest landmark in the area and behind it Luing, where my trip started. On the right is Garbh, no sunbathing today, and, to the left Lunga, my final island, which I shall visit tomorrow.

A boat full of tourists passes by, completely oblivious of this breath-taking island. They hardly give Garbh a second look, inspired instead by their tunnel vision fascination for the Corryvreckan. Two gulls float above me, enjoying this magnificent spring day. Even from up here I can hear the sounds of the sea, gently lapping against the rocks below.

I walk back down towards the raised beach. Surrounded by heather, with pebbles in its centre, it looks as though it has suffered at the hands of a TV makeover artist. Although it strikes me as strangely bizarre in such surroundings, it certainly has its own beauty. I head south and come across a cave. Rocky on one side, there is quartz on the other wall and inside a raised platform that is covered with heather. It looks as though it has served as a bed at some time.

Soon it will be time to watch the sunset. I return to my tent, fetch my bottle of malt, switch on Radio 2 and let my thoughts wander.

It is time for Johnnie Walker's traffic report. "And now it's over to Dubh Mor for the latest traffic update. Well Johnnie, today on Dubh Mor we have no boats sailing, but ten sheep are moving in a slow convoy along the raised beach and one stationary human being is getting pissed in front of his tent with a teddy bear."

95% of the moon is now over Lunga and the sun is sinking slowly south of Garbh. The sky is light blue and there are faint white clouds in the distance. An aeroplane is flying straight up into the sky, pointing directly towards them. Following behind, in two white lines of smoke, is a gull.

These islands are going to change my life forever. How, I have no idea. But, one day, I hope that I will move to Scotland, to be nearer to them. Deep within my heart, I know I'd love to live on one of these glorious islands. To me they are my destiny, my life and my purpose.

The sun sets just after 8.00pm. Finally, the land and the islands become black, and the sea starts to shimmer from the intensity of a magnificent kaleidoscope of colours in the sky. The whisky is finished. It is time for me to return to my tent and allow this beautiful island to embrace me as I fall sleep.

I awaken feeling decidedly fuzzy after last night's drunkenness. Hamish and his parents arrive at 8.30am for my last drop off. They, especially Hamish, have been tremendous and the camaraderie has been great.

In no time at all, we have arrived at Lunga, island number 42. Being in no rush, we rest awhile in the water, to finish our coffee and enjoy a yarn. I land onto rocks at Port an Tigh-airigh, on the east side of the island. There's an old house nearby, which is still hanging on as the island bothy. I set up camp in front of it.

Today I am physically knackered. I lie inside my tent for ages. As I rest, I realise that mentally I am spent. These eight islands are not easy, all hills, bogs, rock, with very few tracks. Yet they have been a major chunk to get under my belt, as well as giving me vital experience. I remember how I felt getting onto Hamish's boat that first day. Now I am much more experienced, and to sleep solo on uninhabited islands no longer holds any fear for me. I feel that I have earned my stripes on this trip.

In some ways Dubh Mor has been my favourite, although each island has its own individual appeal. Lunga appears beautiful too, but I know I'm beat. At the moment, a Cal Mac ferry and a pier sounds really nice, just like a holiday.

Right now, I could definitely appreciate some creature comforts.

Until now, my health has been perfect this month. But today, not only has my physical energy vanished, I have also found two ticks. Ticks are like lice with long legs and I have one behind each knee joint. Eventually I manage to pull them out. It isn't easy as the little bastards kept hanging on.

By 1.30pm, the sun is high in the cloudless sky. It is time to go walkabout. Using my final blast of energy, I set off walking to the top of Bidein na h-Iolaire, which at 98 metres, is the highest point on Lunga. It is worth the effort. From the top, the last week of islands lie before me and in the distance, the Colonsay ferry is sailing beyond the Garvellachs. How I would love to be sitting on it just now, enjoying a beer and a plate of chips.

Clyde has his final photo taken. Then slowly, exhausted, we head back to camp. My spirits are low; I am going home. Yet, I know that realistically, this is the only sensible option. I am worn out, I have nothing left. I need to go home, to rest and recuperate.

I wonder if those ticks jumped on me in that stream on Garbh?

Back at my tent, I begin to get my kit ready for the morning and then hit my sleeping bag.

I awake to the sun rising golden orange, forcing its way through a grey sky. I am packed and ready in good time for Hamish to arrive. As I stand waiting for him at the water's edge, I experience my final and possibly greatest joy of this trip. I catch sight of an otter, going about its business between the rocks and shallow water. This spectacle fills me with such excitement and reminds me that, strangely enough, I haven't seen one seal around these eight islands.

After finally bidding goodbye to Hamish and his family, I walk up the pontoon only to be called back again. I have left my tent! The first left luggage of the nine days. Now, back on the mainland, my brain has gone into auto-pilot.

My car feels warm and welcoming, although I am itching from my countless bites and lack of a shower. Quickly I call Ruth and head straight for home.

Ruth runs out to greet me. She is greeted by an insistent "Don't touch me!" I have this image of whatever is crawling over me, jumping onto her! So, after a quick peck on the cheek, I throw my clothes into the washing machine and dive into the shower.

Food and sex are the essence of any young man's life, but you can forget that for now. I stand in the shower and let the water trickle over me. It is so good to have hot water. I shampoo my hair and my skin starts to breathe again.

120 islands still await me.

Appendix 2 - List of Islands Slept On

Slept On Number	Island Name	Date Slept On	Inhabited Number*	Uninhabited Number*
1	Barra	06/09/03	1	
2	Eigg	11/09/03	2	
3	Rum	15/09/03	3	
4	Canna	17/09/03	4	
5	Ulva	22/09/03	5	
6	Iona	25/09/03	6	
7	Colonsay	26/12/03	7	
8	Graemsay	02/04/04	8	
9	Shapinsay	03/04/04	9	
10	North Ronaldsay	05/04/04	10	
11	Wyre	08/04/04	11	
12	Egilsay	09/04/04	12	
13	Papa Westray	10/04/04	13	
14	Westray	12/04/04	14	
15	Rousay	14/04/04	15	
16	Shetland Mainland	06/06/04	16	
17	Foula	08/06/04	17	
18	Muck	12/10/04	18	
19	Kerrera	18/10/04	19	
20	Luing	22/03/05	20	
21	Carna	24/03/05		1
22	Lismore	25/03/05	21	
23	Great Cumbrae	26/03/05	22	
24	Little Cumbrae	27/03/05	23	
25	Bute	28/03/05	24	
26	Inchmarnock	30/03/05		2
27	Arran	31/03/05	25	
28	Holy Island	01/04/05	26	
29	Gigha	02/04/05	27	
30	Cara	03/04/05		3
31	Islay	05/04/05	28	
32	Jura	06/04/05	29	
33	Mull	08/04/05	30	
34	Sanda	11/04/05	31	
35	Scarba	14/04/05		4
36	Naoimh	15/04/05		5
37	Shuna	16/04/05	32	
38	Macaskin	17/04/05		6
39	Righ	18/04/05		7
40	Garbh	19/04/05		8
41	Dubh Mor	20/04/05		9
42	Lunga	21/04/05		10

*Inhabited and Uninhabited numbers are the cumulative frequency of each type of island.